
**If you have a problem with Game Genie,™ call the
GAME GENIE HELPLINE for immediate assistance:**
1-513-868-8835
NEW CODES NOT AVAILABLE BY PHONE.
SEE BACK PAGE FOR CODE UPDATE OFFER!

Introducing Game Genie™ Video Game Enhancer

With Game Genie video game enhancer, you can program your video games to change certain game-play features on many popular titles for the Nintendo Entertainment System®.

The changes you make with Game Genie are not permanent, and disappear when the power to the game deck is turned off. When connected properly, Game Genie will not damage either your game cartridges or your game deck.

Game Genie is a cartridge-like pack that connects between your game cartridge and the game deck. It introduces its own startup screen, called the "Code Screen," when you power up your game deck. On this screen, you enter special codes from examples listed in this manual for modifying game-play features (games appear in alphabetical order beginning on page 16). Or you can program your own codes.

Up to three codes can be entered at the same time. Some advanced game-play changes require more than one code to be entered.

Before you begin entering codes, you must properly connect the Game Genie unit.

The Nintendo® Control Deck™ should be connected normally, following the instructions that came with it. TURN OFF THE POWER TO THE GAME DECK BEFORE PLUGGING IN THE GAME GENIE UNIT.

If you have a problem with Game Genie,™ call the GAME GENIE HELPLINE for immediate assistance:

1-513-868-8835

NEW CODES NOT AVAILABLE BY PHONE.

SEE BACK PAGE FOR CODE UPDATE OFFER!

DIRT HURTS!

DIRT in the connectors of your NES® deck, game cart or Game Genie™ can cause game play problems!

If you have any of the following PROBLEMS, CLEANING the deck, game cart and Game Genie connectors could easily solve them!

- **GAME STOPS OR SCREEN "FREEZES"**
- **DISTORTED OR "SCRAMBLED" SCREEN**

We recommend regular use of a CLEANING KIT such as the NES Cleaning Kit™. Follow the instructions that come with the kit.

USE THE CLEANING KIT TO CLEAN *BOTH ENDS* OF THE GAME GENIE.

Clean the black connector using the tool supplied in the cleaning kit for cleaning the NES Deck. Clean the other end using the tool supplied for cleaning the game cart.

KEEP YOUR GAME GENIE™ CLEAN. Always store it in the box.

Consult the Troubleshooting Guide on Page 11 for more information.

NES and NES Cleaning Kit are trademarks of Nintendo of America, Inc.
Game Genie is a trademark of Lewis Galoob Toys, Inc.

Connecting the Game Cart

1) Carefully plug your game cartridge all the way onto the black connector on the Game Genie so that the Game Genie handle overlaps the top (label) side of the game cartridge. (Figures 1 and 2)

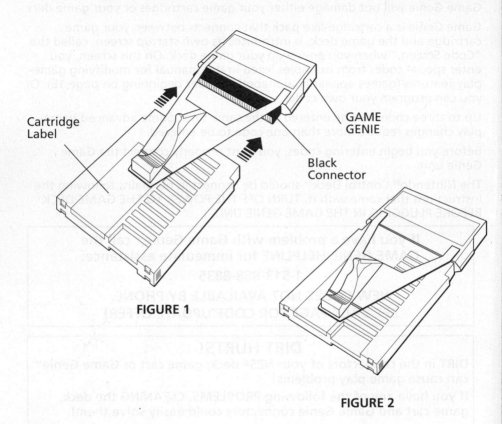

Cartridge Label

GAME GENIE

Black Connector

FIGURE 1

FIGURE 2

Connecting Game Genie

1) TURN OFF THE POWER TO THE GAME DECK BEFORE PLUGGING IN THE GAME GENIE UNIT.

2) Plug the Game Genie (with game cart attached) into the deck as you would an ordinary game cart. Grasping the game cartridge, push the Game Genie carefully but firmly all the way into the deck until the wedge on the handle touches the lid of the deck. (Figure 3)

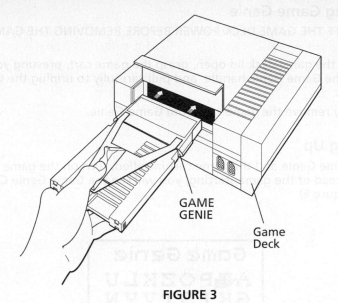

GAME
GENIE

Game
Deck

FIGURE 3

The lid should close down to meet the "Close Line" on the Game Genie handle. (Figures 4 and 5)

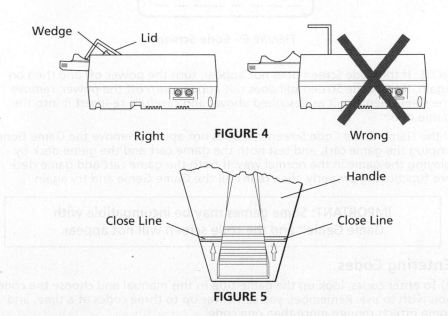

Wedge　　Lid

Right　　**FIGURE 4**　　Wrong

Handle

Close Line　　　　Close Line

FIGURE 5

If the lid does not meet the "Close Line," or the deck lid does not close, remove the Game Genie unit as decribed in the next section, and re-insert it as described above.

Removing Game Genie

1) TURN OFF THE GAME DECK POWER BEFORE REMOVING THE GAME GENIE UNIT.

2) Holding the game deck lid open, grasp the game cart, pressing your thumb down on the Game Genie handle, and pull carefully to unplug the Game Genie unit.

3) Carefully remove the game cart from Game Genie.

Powering Up

1) With Game Genie and the game cart installed, turn on the game deck power. Instead of the game starting, you will see the Game Genie Code Screen. (Figure 6)

FIGURE 6 - Code Screen

NOTE: If the Code Screen does not appear, turn the power off and then on again. If the Code Screen still does not appear, turn off the power, remove the Game Genie unit as described above, and carefully re-insert it into the game deck.

If the Game Genie Code Screen still does not appear, remove the Game Genie, unplug the game cart, and test both the game cart and the game deck by playing the game in the normal way. If both the game cart and game deck are functioning properly, then re-install the Game Genie and try again.

IMPORTANT: Some games may be incompatible with Game Genie™ and the code screen will not appear.

Entering Codes

1) To enter codes, look up the game title in this manual and choose the codes you wish to use. Remember, you can enter up to three codes at a time, and some effects require more than one code.

2) To enter codes on the Code Screen, use the control pad on the number 1 Nintendo® controller. The two lines of letters in the top portion of the screen

are the Letter Choices that make up the codes. You will see a hand on the screen pointing to the Letter Choice "A" in the top left corner of the screen. The 3 rows of blank spaces are the Code Lines. The "swirling star" cursor will appear on the first space of the top Code Line. (Figure 7)

FIGURE 7

Note: If you are using a special controller and are having difficulty entering Game Genie codes, use the standard controller that came with your Nintendo® deck to enter the codes, and then replace it with the special controller to play the game. If you are using a light gun, plug it into Port 2 and your controller into Port 1. Use the controller to enter codes and the light gun to play the game.

3) Move the hand to point to the first Letter Choice of the code by pressing UP, DOWN, LEFT and RIGHT on the control pad.

4) PRESS THE "A" BUTTON TO ENTER THE LETTER ON THE CODE LINE. The "swirling star" cursor will move to the next space on the Code Line. Continue in this way until all the code letters have been entered. You have now entered the first code.

5) The completed Code Line will dim, and the "swirling star" will move to the first space on the next Code Line.

6) Repeat this procedure to enter up to three codes, if desired.

Correcting Mistakes

1) If you make a mistake and enter the wrong letter, press the "B" button to delete the last letter entered. Then enter the correct letter as described in steps 3 and 4 in the previous section.

2) Or, you can move the cursor (the "swirling star") to any previously entered letter on the Code Lines by moving the hand down to the Code Line, pointing the hand at the letter you want to change, and pressing the "A" button. The letter you want to replace will be highlighted. Then you can enter a new letter by moving the hand back up to the desired Letter Choice and pressing "A" again. Repeat this procedure to change any other entered letters.

3) To return to the space in the Code Line where you were, move the hand back to the space, press "A" to highlight the space, and then move the hand back up to the Letter Choices to continue entering codes.

Starting the Game

WHEN ALL DESIRED CODES HAVE BEEN ENTERED, DOUBLE-CHECK THEM TO ENSURE THEY HAVE BEEN ENTERED CORRECTLY. Then press "Start" on the controller to begin the game. The first screen of the game will appear normally. Proceed to play the game as usual, according to the instructions that came with it.

To return to the Game Genie Code Screen from the game at any time, turn off the power to the deck and then turn it on again.

If you want to play the game again and keep the codes in effect, simply press "Reset."

If you want to play the game normally without entering any codes, you do not have to remove the Game Genie unit. Just press "Start" with no codes entered on the Code Screen.

If You Have Problems with Codes. . .

Every effort has been made to test and verify each code listed in this book. However, it is possible that some codes or combinations of codes may cause undesired effects at some point in the game play. If this occurs, it will not harm your games or deck.

Simply shut off the power to the game deck and turn it back on again to bring up the Code Screen.

◆ Double-check to make sure you enter the codes correctly.

◆ If the problem occurred when using a single code, enter a different code.

◆ If the problem occurred when using a combination of codes, try entering them in a different order or trying a new combination of codes.

◆ Entering passwords and Game Genie codes together may cause problems in some games.

◆ Start the game again.

If you have a problem with Game Genie,™ call the
GAME GENIE HELPLINE for immediate assistance:
1-513-868-8835
NEW CODES NOT AVAILABLE BY PHONE.
SEE BACK PAGE FOR CODE UPDATE OFFER!

If you come across a code or combination of codes that causes an interruption or other undesired effect in a game, please write to us at the address below. Be sure to include your name, age, address and phone number, along with the problem code(s) and a brief description of the problem. Your observations can help us to improve future editions of the Codebook.

Game Genie Consumer Service
2350 Pleasant Avenue
Hamilton, OH 45015

Troubleshooting Guide

PROBLEM	REMEDY
Game "freezes," stops, or interrupts	◆ CLEAN METAL CONTACTS ON DECK, GAME GENIE AND GAME CART CONNECTORS USING A CLEANING KIT SUCH AS NES CLEANING KIT™. ◆ Problem code. WILL NOT HARM GAME. Turn power off and on and re-enter codes. If using a single code, choose another code. If using 2 or 3 codes, enter them in a different order, or try a different combination of codes.
No picture	◆ Make sure TV and Nintendo® deck are plugged in. ◆ Make sure TV and deck are turned on. ◆ Make sure TV and deck are connected properly. Refer to NES™ instructions. ◆ Make sure Channel 3/4 switch on deck is set correctly. Refer to NES™ instructions. ◆ Remove Game Genie, insert game cart into deck and test normal operation of game and deck. If problem occurs without Game Genie, refer to NES instructions. ◆ CLEAN METAL CONTACTS ON DECK, GAME GENIE AND GAME CART CONNECTORS USING A CLEANING KIT SUCH AS NES CLEANING KIT™.
Game Genie™ Code Screen does not appear	◆ Turn deck power off and then on again. ◆ Remove Game Genie and reinsert firmly into deck. Deck door should close down onto "Close Line" on Game Genie handle. (See page 7.) ◆ Remove Game Genie, unplug game cart from Game Genie and carefully but firmly reconnect. Reinsert Game Genie into deck. ◆ Remove Game Genie, insert game cart into deck and test normal operation of game and deck. (See "No Picture," above.) ◆ CLEAN METAL CONTACTS ON DECK, GAME GENIE AND GAME CART CONNECTORS USING A CLEANING KIT SUCH AS NES CLEANING KIT™.
No picture or Code Screen some of the time	◆ Game may be incompatible with Game Genie. Play a different game. ◆ CLEAN METAL CONTACTS ON DECK, GAME GENIE AND GAME CART CONNECTORS USING A CLEANING KIT SUCH AS NES CLEANING KIT™. ◆ Poor connection of Game Genie, game cart and/or deck. Repeat connection procedures.
Hard to push Game Genie into game cart	◆ This is normal, expecially when Game Genie is new, and WILL NOT HARM THE GAME CART.
"Scraping" noise when pushing Game Genie into deck chamber	◆ This is normal, expecially when Game Genie is new, and WILL NOT HARM THE GAME DECK.
Hard to push Game Genie into deck chamber	◆ This is normal. Push the Game Genie into the deck firmly. After several times, you will get the hang of it.
Unintended effect that does not interrupt game	◆ Problem code. WILL NOT HARM GAME. Either continue play or turn power off and on and re-enter codes. If using a single code, choose another code. If using 2 or 3 codes, enter them in a different order, or try a different combination of codes.
Any other problem	◆ Call GAME GENIE HELPLINE for assistance at 1-513-868-8835.

Programming Your Own Codes

The codes listed in this manual give you an idea of the kinds of effects you can create by programming your own codes to enhance game play and add to your enjoyment.

When programming your own codes, keep in mind the following guidelines:

◆ The easiest way to program your own codes is to make slight changes in existing codes. In the next section, there are simple tables that show you how to change the example codes in the manual to create effects you might enjoy.

◆ If you are making small changes to existing codes, it is best to leave the same number of letters in the code.

◆ You can also program codes by simply using random letters. The best results are obtained when you make up codes of 6 letters.

◆ Using 3 codes at a time makes it more likely to get an effect, but it's a more difficult way to program random codes, since it's harder to tell which code is making the effect happen.

◆ Most codes of the proper length will have some effect, but often it will be such a small change that you will not even notice any difference. You may have to try many random codes before you get an interesting effect.

◆ If you find a random code that has an interesting effect, then try changing it by using the programming techniques in the next section. This way, you are more likely to "home in" on a really good effect.

Your success in code programming will depend a lot on luck. Keep trying! Of course, some of the effects you create you may not like. Almost any effect is possible—good, bad, interesting, annoying, fun, or just plain silly.

If a code you program interrupts the game or causes an undesired effect, just turn off the power and turn it on again, and then program different codes to play.

How to Program

There are two basic methods used to program your own codes by changing existing codes.

Using Method #1, you change either the **first** or **second** letter of the code. Using Method #2, you change either the **first** or **last** letter of the code.

You can also combine both methods if you wish.

Method #1 and Method #2 will work best on **single codes**, when the effect of the code you wish to change has **numbers** in it (for example, number of lives, number of bullets, number of weapons, number of seconds or minutes on the timer).

The best way to proceed is to write down the original code, look up the choices in the tables below, and then write down all the variations below the original code. This way, you can return to your Game Genie™ with your own list of codes to try.

Reminder: If a code you program interrupts the game or causes an undesired effect, just turn off the power and turn it on again, and then program different codes to play.

Method #1

Using Method #1, you change either the **first** or **second** letter of the original code. First try changing the first letter and write down the new code. Then try changing the second. Then try changing both the first and second at the same time.

How to use the tables: Find the letter you want to change in one of the tables. Then substitute one of the other letters **in the same table**.

The farther apart two letters are in the table, the bigger the change in the effect will be. For example, in Table 1, changing **A** to **Y** will make a bigger difference than changing **A** to **Z**. In Table 2, changing **V** to **O** will make a bigger difference than changing **V** to **S**.

Table 1	A P Z L G I T Y

EXAMPLE: If the first or second letter of the code is **P**, you can change it to **A, Z, L, G, I, T** or **Y**. Try them all!

Table 2	E O X U K S V N

EXAMPLE: If the first or second letter of the code is **U**, you can change it to **E, O, X, K, S, V** or **N**. Try them all!

SAMPLES FOR METHOD #1: The Game Genie™ example Code 6 for **Super Mario Bros.**™ Game is **A P Z L G K**, which allows Mario™ to jump higher when he's not running. Using Method #1, look up the first letter (**A**) in the tables. In Table 1, you find the **A**. One of the letters you can substitute for **A** is **L**.

Original code   **A** P Z L G K   Using Table 1   **L** P Z L G K

Then look up the second letter, **P**. You find **P** in Table 1 also. **G** is one of the letters you can substitute for **P**.

Original code   A **P** Z L G K   Using Table 1   A **G** Z L G K

Try combining these last two examples. See what you get!

Super Mario Bros. and Mario are trademarks of Nintendo of America Inc.

The Game Genie™ example Code 3 for **Snake, Rattle 'N' Roll**™ Game is **E P N N V X T T**, which allows you to slow down the timer. Using Method #1, look up the first letter, E, in the tables. In Table 2, you find the E. One of the letters you can substitute for E is X.

Original code   **E** P N N V X T T   Using Table 2   **X** P N N V X T T

Then look up the second letter, **P**. You find P in Table 1. Z is one of the letters you can substitute for P.

Original code   E **P** N N V X T T   Using Table 1   E **Z** N N V X T T

Try combining the last two examples. See what you get!

Snake, Rattle 'n' Roll is a trademark of Nintendo of America Inc.

Method #2

In Method #2, you change either the **first** or **last** letter of the original code. First try changing the first letter. Then try changing the last. Then try changing both the first and last at the same time.

How to use the table: Find the letter you want to change in the table and change it to the letter on its right.

Table 3

A	can be changed to	E	G	can be changed to	K
E	can be changed to	A	K	can be changed to	G
P	can be changed to	O	I	can be changed to	S
O	can be changed to	P	S	can be changed to	I
Z	can be changed to	X	T	can be changed to	V
X	can be changed to	Z	V	can be changed to	T
L	can be changed to	U	Y	can be changed to	N
U	can be changed to	L	N	can be changed to	Y

EXAMPLES: If the first letter of the code is **O**, you can change it to **P**. If the last letter of the code is **Y**, you can change it to **N**.

SAMPLES FOR METHOD #2: Go back to Game Genie™ sample Code 6 for **Super Mario Bros.**™ Game, **A P Z L G K**. Looking up the first letter, **A**, you see that **A** can be changed to **E**.

Original code **A** P Z L G K   Using Table 3 **E** P Z L G K

Looking up the last letter, **K**, you see that **K** can be changed to **G**.

Original code A P Z L G **K**   Using Table 3 E P Z L G **G**

Try combining these last two examples. See what you get!

And, using both Methods #1 and #2, you could come up with a code like:

Original code **A** P Z L G **K**   Using both methods **Z** P Z L G **G**

See if you can figure out how this one was done!

Super Mario Bros. is a trademark of Nintendo of America Inc.

Let's go back to the Game Genie™ example Code 3 for **Snake, Rattle 'N' Roll**™ Game, **E P N N V X T T**. Look up the last letter, **T**. You find that **T** can be changed to **V**.

Original code E P N N V X T **T**   Using Table 3 E P N N V X T **V**

Remember, programming is an art that requires lots of patient, trial-and-error experimenting! The techniques will not work on all codes, but keep trying until you discover a code that works. Of course, the methods we've described are not the only ones that might work. Feel free to invent your own programming techniques!

There are many different types of codes you can use to change game-play features with Game Genie™ video game enhancer. For quick reference, find the symbol for the type of code you want to use on this page. Then turn to the game codes in the listings on the follow-ing pages (games appear in alphabetical order) and look for the symbol next to the corresponding code or codes.

Ammunition

Energy/
Food/
Fuel

Extra
Continues/
Credits

Handicap

Infinite Lives

Invincibility/
Protection

Keep Weapons/
Equipment/
Power-Ups

Lives

Magic!

In-Game
Money/
Currency

Mega Power
(and sometimes
Infinite Lives)

Super
Mega Power

Speed

Super Flying

Super/Mega
Jumping

Timer

Weapons/
Equipment

World, Level
and Stage
Warps

Mystery/Weird/
Special/Defies
Categories

1942™ Game

1942™ is a great game, but what if your friend isn't as good as you are? The Game Genie™ can provide the answer. Why not give one player more lives than the other? '42 Codes 6 and 7 will let you do this. You can also use '42 Codes 2 and 3 to change the number of lives you have in a one-player game. Have fun!

'42

CODE	KEY IN . . .	EFFECT . . .	
1	PASIOALE	Both players start with 9 rolls	
2	IESUTYZA	Player 1 starts with 9 lives	
3	AESUTYZE	Player 2 starts with 9 lives	
4	IAKUUAZA	After continue, player 1 has 6 lives in 2-player game	
5	AAKUUAZE	After continue, player 1 has 9 lives in 2-player game	
6	IASUOAZA	Player 2 has 6 lives in 2-player game	
7	AASUOAZE	Player 2 has 9 lives in 2-player game	

Remember that you can pick'n'mix your codes! You can enter up to THREE separate codes at one time.

1942 is a trademark of Capcom USA, Inc.
Game Genie is a trademark of Lewis Galoob Toys, Inc.

1943™ Game

Aw, come on! I could really use a few more points to power up my P-38 . . . whatsat? The Game Genie™ has the answer? Why yes, yes it does! Just use '43 Codes 1 through 3 to choose how many points you want. And of course now that you're a bit more "beefed up," you'll want to warp to the later levels. Just use '43 Codes 4 through 7 to do that!

'43

CODE	KEY IN . . .	EFFECT . . .	
1	ZESNLLLE	10 power points	
2	GOSNLLLA	20 power points	
3	TOSNLLLE	30 power points	
4	AEVYZLAE	Start on mission 5	
5	ZOVYZLAA	Start on mission 10	
6	GOVYZLAE	Start on mission 15	
7	TXVYZLAA	Start on mission 20	

Remember, you can program your own codes! '43 Codes 1 through 3 might make good codes to try your programming luck on!

1943 is a trademark of Capcom USA, Inc.
Game Genie is a trademark of Lewis Galoob Toys, Inc.

3D Worldrunner™ Game

We thought that WorldRunner™ may want a little help if he's going to liberate 8 planets today ` . . . 3D Code 8 should give you a competitive advantage. Also, try 3D Code 9 to save wearing out your thumb!

3D

CODE	KEY IN . . .	EFFECT . . .	
1	AEUOLTPA	Infinite lives	

Some codes may cause undesired effects (which are not permanent). If this occurs,

2	PEUPPTLA + PLVOLTLL	Start with 1 life	
3	TEUPPTLA + TLVOLTLL	Start with 6 lives	
4	PEUPPTLE + PLVOLTLU	Start with 9 lives	
5	SXUPZGVG	Freeze timer	
6	NNXOYGEK	Slow down timer	
7	AVXOYGEG	Speed up timer	
8	AEUOVIGA	Start with and keep laser missiles	
9	OXUONISX	Autofire	
10	XZEAUOOZ + PAEAKPAA + VAEASPSA	Start on world 2	
11	XZEAUOOZ + ZAEAKPAA + VAEASPSA	Start on world 3	
12	XZEAUOOZ + LAEAKPAA + VAEASPSA	Start on world 4	
13	XZEAUOOZ + GAEAKPAA + VAEASPSA	Start on world 5	
14	XZEAUOOZ + IAEAKPAA + VAEASPSA	Start on world 6	
15	XZEAUOOZ + TAEAKPAA + VAEASPSA	Start on world 7	

You can use up to three codes each time you play, but mixing codes with opposite effects will not work—like 3D Codes 6 and 7.

3D WorldRunner and WorldRunner are trademarks of Acclaim Entertainment, Inc.

720 Degrees™ Game

To be really good at this game you need to practice—lots! Why not try 720 Code 1 for a while, and when you are ready, play with no codes at all to see if you are a better skater. You don't have to remove the Game Genie™ to play with no codes at all—just press START without entering any codes.

720 CODE	KEY IN . . .	EFFECT . . .	
1	SZUYASVK	Infinite continues	
2	PEXKLZLE	9 continues	
3	TEXKLZLA	6 continues	
4	PEXKLZLA	No continues, instead of usual 2	
5	GEKKYZAA	Start with all equipment	
6	ZEKKYZAA	Start with half equipment	
7	XVXGGXSX + OXXGIXTE + ZEXGTZZA	Start on level 2	
8	XVXGGXSX + OXXGIXTE + LEXGTZZA	Start on level 3	
9	XVXGGXSX + OXXGIXTE + GEXGTZZA	Start on level 4	

Remember that you can pick'n'mix your codes! You can enter up to THREE single codes at one time, or one triple-code like 720 Code 7.

720 Degrees is a trademark of Atari Games Corp. Used by Mindscape Inc. under license.
Game Genie is a trademark of Lewis Galoob Toys, Inc.

8 Eyes™ Game

EYE Codes 1 and 2 will help keep you safe from those nasty nuclear mutants, and EYE Codes 3 and 4 give you a nice head start. EYE Codes 5 and 6 used together make a very powerful combination that should teach those Dukes™ a thing or two.

EYE CODE	KEY IN . . .	EFFECT . . .
1	GXOUSUSE	Most attacks won't damage Orin™
2	GXNGNOSE	Most attacks won't damage Cutrus™
3	AGVXGXYZ	Start with more energy—Orin
4	AGVXIXYZ	Start with more energy—Cutrus
5	YZVXTZAE	Start game with some item power
6	GXSLKVSE	Never lose item power once gained
7	VTOVNTVA	Start game with dagger

Remember that you can pick'n'mix your codes—you can enter up to THREE separate EYE Codes at the same time.

8 Eyes, Dukes, Orin and Cutrus are trademarks of Taxan USA Corp.

Adventure Island II™ Game

Some excellent codes here to help Master Higgins™ in this great new adventure! Of course, there's infinite lives and infinite energy. There's also ISL2 Code 6 to make that skateboard easier to ride. And now you can skate backwards too! ISL2 Code 8 stops you from losing energy bars when you crash into things like rocks and walls. It really comes in handy for exploring those caves! There's plenty more codes too, so choose your favorites and go for it, Islanders!

ISL2 CODE	KEY IN . . .	EFFECT . . .
1	PEXVAALA	1 extra life
2	TEXVAALA	6 extra lives
3	PEXVAALE	9 extra lives
4	SXNLOKVK	Infinite lives
5	SZUIGEVK	Infinite energy
6	AENZTPAZ	Reversible skateboard
7	ALKXAAAZ	Faster running
8	AAKSEYZA	Don't lose energy from hitting objects
9	SXSUAOSU + GEXULGPA	Higher jump

Remember that you can pick'n'mix your codes.

Adventure Island II and Master Higgins are trademarks of Hudson Soft USA, Inc.

Adventures In The Magic Kingdom™ Game

MAGIC Codes 1 thru 8 let you alter the cost of any of the option screen items, making the game harder or easier to suit your ability. MAGIC Code 9 lets you have items for free! And MAGIC Code 13 stops you from losing your lives in the 'attractions'.

Some codes may cause undesired effects (which are not permanent). If this occurs,

MAGIC CODE	KEY IN . . .	EFFECT . . .
1	LAKUTGTA	'Life' costs less
2	GAKUTGTE	'Life' costs more
3	GAKUYKAA	'Freeze' costs less
4	YAKUYKAE	'Freeze' costs more
5	IASLAKZA	'Invincible' costs less
6	GPSLAKZA	'Invincible' costs more
7	TASLPKGA	'Life Up' costs less
8	APSLPKGE	'Life Up' costs more
9	GXELLXSN + AAXUAXGY	All items for free!
10	PEVEIALA	Start with 1 life
11	TEVEIALA	Start with 6 lives
12	PEVEIALE	Start with 9 lives
13	SXKYUOVK	Never lose a life in 'attractions'
14	NYKULZKU	More 'Freeze' time
15	AGKULZKL	Less 'Freeze' time
16	EGSUYXGL	More 'Invincible' time
17	SZSTGVVK	Infinite candles
18	EYKVNKXN	Mega-jump

Remember that you can pick'n'mix your codes.

Adventures In The Magic Kingdom is a trademark of The Walt Disney Company. Used by Capcom USA, Inc. under license.

The Adventures of Bayou Billy™ Game

You can help your Cajun friend in his adventures by giving him more lives and/or more energy. You can have infinite lives with BILL Code 1, or infinite energy with BILL Code 2. You can also start at whatever level you like by using BILL Codes 6 thru 12—but since they each take three codes, you can't use any others at the same time!

BILL CODE	KEY IN . . .	EFFECT . . .
1	GZOVLLVG	Infinite lives
2	PEKVIZYA + SXOOUKVK	Infinite energy
3	AAETAGZA	Start with 1 life
4	IAETAGZA	Start with 6 lives
5	AAETAGZE	Start with 9 lives
6	PAEVZGAA + UYEVGKPU + AAEVAGGA	Start on level 2
7	ZAEVZGAA + UYEVGKPU + AAEVAGGA	Start on level 3
8	LAEVZGAA + UYEVGKPU + AAEVAGGA	Start on level 4
9	GAEVZGAA + UYEVGKPU + AAEVAGGA	Start on level 5
10	IAEVZGAA + UYEVGKPU + AAEVAGGA	Start on level 6
11	TAEVZGAA + UYEVGKPU + AAEVAGGA	Start on level 7
12	YAEVZGAA + UYEVGKPU + AAEVAGGA	Start on level 8

Remember that you can pick'n'mix your codes! You can enter any of the level warps (BILL Codes 6 thru 12) alone, or a mixture of the other BILL Codes.

The Adventures of Bayou Billy is a trademark of Konami Inc.

Adventures of Dino-Riki™ Game

There are lots of Game Genie™ codes for Dino-Riki™—look down the list. You have stage warps, extra lives, infinite lives, and extra life hearts. The star code for this game is DINO Code 8, which makes sure that he starts off as Macho-Riki™ and stays that way regardless of what happens. Try RIKI Codes 1 and 5 together to see all of the game in one session.

DINO CODE	KEY IN . . .	EFFECT . . .	
1	SZEETTVG	Start with infinite lives	
2	AESEPGZA	Start with 1 life	
3	IESEPGZA	Start with 6 lives	
4	AESEPGZE	Start with 9 lives	
5	SZUENZVG	Start with infinite life hearts	
6	GESEIGZA	Start with 4 life hearts	
7	AESEIGZE	Start with 8 life hearts	
8	VKEAPISA	Start Macho (big), stay Macho	
9	VVEAPISA	Start as Macho-Riki	
10	IEVASPIG	Once Macho, stay Macho	
11	TKSAAGSA + ZEKEIGAA	Start on stage 2-1	
12	TKSAAGSA + GEKEIGAA	Start on stage 3-1	
13	TKSAAGSA + TEKEIGAA	Start on stage 4-1	
14	TKSAAGSA + AEKEIGAE	Start on stage 4-2	
15	TKSAAGSA + ZEKEIGAE	Start on stage 4-3	
16	TKSAAGSA + GEKEIGAE	Start on stage 4-4	

Remember, you can program your own codes! DINO Codes 2 through and 4 and 6 and 7 might make good codes to try your programming luck on!

Adventures of Dino-Riki, Dino-Riki and Macho-Riki are trademarks of Hudson Soft USA, Inc.
Game Genie is a trademark of Lewis Galoob Toys, Inc.

Adventures of Lolo™ Game

You can make the game harder or easier by using LOL Codes 2 or 3, or you can explore the game with LOL Code 1.

LOL CODE	KEY IN . . .	EFFECT . . .	
1	SXOPSPVG	Infinite lives	
2	PEKPOAIA	1 life for Lolo	
3	PEKPOAIE	9 lives for Lolo	

Remember, you can program your own codes! LOL Codes 2 and 3 might make good codes to try your programming luck on!

Adventures of Lolo is a trademark of HAL America, Inc.

Adventures of Lolo 2™ Game

Your little friend Lolo™ can start the game with a few magic shots in hand by using LOLO Codes 5 and 6. You can also use LOLO Code 7 to make sure that you never lose your magic shots—the game forgets to count how many you've used, so in effect you have infinite magic shots!

Some codes may cause undesired effects (which are not permanent). If this occurs,

LOLO
CODE   KEY IN . . .   EFFECT . . .

CODE	KEY IN ...	EFFECT ...
1	GZXPVLVG	Infinite lives
2	PESPXPIA	Start with 1 life
3	ZESPXPIE	Start with 10 lives
4	YESPXPIE	Start with 15 lives
5	ZAEPSZAA	Start with 2 magic shots
6	GAEPSZAA	Start with 4 magic shots
7	GXNXUAVG	Never lose magic shots
8	GEUPKPAA	Start at world 5
9	PEUPKPAE	Start at world 10
10	TEUPKPAE	Start at world 15
11	LOUPKPAA	Start at world 20
12	AOUPKPAE	Start at world 25
13	IOUPKPAE	Start at world 30

Remember that you can pick'n'mix your codes—you can enter up to THREE separate LOLO Codes at the same time.

Adventures of Lolo 2 and Lolo are trademarks of HAL America, Inc.

Adventures of Tom Sawyer™ Game

There are lots of brilliant codes for this great game! You can use TOM Codes 2 thru 7 to even out a game where one player is better than the other, or to give Tom a better chance of saving Becky. You can also save the repetition of replaying stages by using TOM Codes 9 thru 18 to go straight to the stage you want!

TOM
CODE   KEY IN . . .   EFFECT . . .

CODE	KEY IN ...	EFFECT ...
1	VZOGGPVG	Infinite Toms
2	PEUZIALA	Player 1 starts with 1 Tom
3	PANXLLLA	Player 2 starts with 1 Tom
4	TEUZIALA	Player 1 starts with 6 Toms
5	TANXLLLA	Player 2 starts with 6 Toms
6	PEUZIALE	Player 1 starts with 9 Toms
7	PANXLLLE	Player 2 starts with 9 Toms
8	IAXGTSZA	Only 5 T's lost from skulls
9	OGSZZSVU	Start at the river—Player 1
10	KISZZSVL	Start in the forest—Player 1
11	NISZZSVU	Start in the house—Player 1
12	XTSZZSVU	Start in the sky—Player 1
13	SYSZZSVL	Start in the cave—Player 1
14	ZEEZALPA + AEEXZLLE	Start at the river—Player 2
15	LEEZALPA + IEEXZLLE	Start in the forest—Player 2
16	GEEZALPA + ZOEXZLLA	Start in the house—Player 2

17	IEEZALPA + YOEXZLLA	Start in the sky—Player 2
18	TEEZALPA + GOEXZLLE	Start in the cave—Player 2

Remember that you can pick'n'mix your codes! You can enter up to THREE separate codes at one time, or one double-code (like TOM Code 14) and one single code (like TOM Code 1).
Adventures of Tom Sawyer is a trademark of SETA USA, Inc.

Air Fortress™ Game

You can have an infinite amount of Beam Bullets™ to help complete the game (FORT Code 6), as well as being able to vary the amount of lives you start with—from 1 life (FORT Code 2) to infinite lives outside the fortress (FORT Code 1), which can change the playability of the game quite a bit. If you have lost the passwords or can't reach the later levels, then use FORT Codes 7 thru 12.

FORT CODE	KEY IN . . .	EFFECT . . .	
1	SZUPKGVG	Infinite lives outside fortress	
2	PAVPKZLA	Start with 1 life	
3	TAVPKZLA	Start with 6 lives	
4	PAVPKZLE	Start with 9 lives	
5	GXKKSIST + GXNKNIST	Don't take damage inside fortress	
6	AAKPSTPA	Infinite Beam Bullets	
7	XZSOXXPZ + PASOUZYA + VASOKZSA	Start on level 2	
8	XZSOXXPZ + ZASOUZYA + VASOKZSA	Start on level 3	
9	XZSOXXPZ + LASOUZYA + VASOKZSA	Start on level 4	
10	XZSOXXPZ + GASOUZYA + VASOKZSA	Start on level 5	
11	XZSOXXPZ + IASOUZYA + VASOKZSA	Start on level 6	
12	XZSOXXPZ + TASOUZYA + VASOKZSA	Start on level 7	
13	APKZNGIA	Pick up double bombs	
14	YYNXUZGV + YNEZEZGV	Pick up extra energy	

Remember, you can program your own codes! FORT Codes 2 through 4 might make good codes to try your programming luck on!
Air Fortress and Beam Bullets are trademarks of HAL America, Inc.

Airwolf™ Game

It takes more than guts . . . a few Game Genie™ codes, perhaps? Even a supersonic jet copter can use a few more missiles—try WOLF Codes 5 thru 9 for truly awesome firepower. The one that we found most useful in this game is WOLF Code 4, which makes the game start at the last level you reached!

WOLF CODE	KEY IN . . .	EFFECT . . .	
1	PAUGVILA	Start with 1 life	
2	TAUGVILA	Start with 6 lives	
3	PAUGVILE	Start with 9 lives	
4	PVXKKKLI	Start at last mission reached	

Some codes may cause undesired effects (which are not permanent). If this occurs,

5	TPVAPXYE	Start with 30 missiles
6	IZVAPXYE	Start with 45 missiles
7	GXSZAPVG	Start with infinite missiles
8	IEVAISYA	Sets missiles to 5 when you refuel
9	TOVAISYE	Sets missiles to 30 when you refuel

Remember that you can pick'n'mix your codes! You can enter up to THREE different WOLF Codes at one time.

Airwolf is a trademark of Universal City Studios, Inc. Used by Acclaim Entertainment, Inc., under license.
Game Genie is a trademark of Lewis Galoob Toys, Inc.

Alien Syndrome™ Game

You have a long list of Game Genie™ codes that enable you to add variety and challenge to this mega-game. SYND Codes 1 and 2 will take the time pressure off you, while SYND Codes 5, 6 and 7 give you a competitive advantage. Not to mention all these others . . .

SYND CODE	KEY IN . . .	EFFECT . . .	
1	SZUNYXVK	Infinite time	
2	GUONPPLL	Set timer to 440	
3	PAOGPIGA	Both players—1 life	
4	AAOGPIGE	Both players—8 lives	
5	PAVKGIAA	Start with flame thrower	
6	ZAVKGIAA	Start with fireball	
7	LAVKGIAA	Start with laser	
8	AEEKXONY	Don't lose life when shot or touched	
9	AANGVXNY	Don't lose life from falling down holes	
10	PEXGGLGA	1 life after continue	
11	AEXGGLGE	8 lives after continue	
12	PENNELAP + KUNNXLAA + LENNULAZ	Start on round 2	
13	ZENNELAP + KUNNXLAA + LENNULAZ	Start on round 3	
14	LENNELAP + KUNNXLAA + LENNULAZ	Start on round 4	
15	GENNELAP + KUNNXLAA + LENNULAZ	Start on round 5	
16	IENNELAP + KUNNXLAA + LENNULAZ	Start on round 6	
17	TENNELAP + KUNNXLAA + LENNULAZ	Start on round 7	

Remember, you can program your own codes! SYND Code 2 might make a good code to try your programming luck on!

Alien Syndrome is a trademark of Sega Enterprises Ltd.
Game Genie is a trademark of Lewis Galoob Toys, Inc.

Alpha Mission™ Game

Keep up the pressure in this exciting shoot'em up—for mega-power use ALFA Codes 5 and 12 together. Also, ALFA Codes 1, 6 and 12 together are pretty powerful . . . try 'em!

ALFA CODE	KEY IN . . .	EFFECT . . .	
1	SXSPYZVG	Infinite lives	
2	PASATLLA	Start with 1 life	
3	TASATLLA	Start with double lives	
4	PASATLLE	Start with triple lives	
5	NYKAYLLE	Start with all weapons available	
6	GZNAILSA	Keep power up after death	
7	GZNAYLSA	Keep energy after death	
8	GAEOUEAA	Thunder uses 25% normal energy	
9	TEXLPTZA	Triple energy gained on 'E' pick-up	
10	ZEULGTGA	Less energy lost on 'Bad E' pick-ups	
11	SZEGGASA	Shield doesn't use energy	
12	IZNAEGSA	You can re-use weapon after selecting	

Remember that you can pick'n'mix your codes! You can enter up to THREE different ALFA Codes at one time.

Alpha Mission is a trademark of SNK Corp. of America

Amagon™ Game

Even the most decorated marine sometimes needs a little backup—these codes can give you a little more in the way of firepower (look at AMA Codes 6 thru 9), just to make sure those monsters don't get you! The star code for this game, however, is AMA Code 4, which gives Amagon™ infinite mega-power!

AMA CODE	KEY IN . . .	EFFECT . . .	
1	AAXGNYPA	Start with infinite lives	
2	PEOVIZGA	Start with 1 life	
3	AEOVIZGE	Start with 8 lives	
4	GZSZIZSP	Infinite mega-power	
5	PEOVPZGA	Start with no bullets!	
6	YEOVPZGA	Start with 600 bullets	
7	AAVYLTPA	Start with infinite bullets	
8	PAVKUIZA	Gain 10 bullets on pick-up	
9	LAVKUIZA	Gain 30 bullets on pick-up	

Remember that you can pick'n'mix your codes! You can enter up to THREE different AMA Codes at one time.

Amagon is a trademark of American Sammy Corporation.

Some codes may cause undesired effects (which are not permanent). If this occurs,

Archon™ Game

These codes give you the advantage over the computer player by allowing you free movement on the chessboard. ARC Code 1 lets your ground travelers move anywhere you want. ARC Code 2 is for your fliers and teleporters. In a two-player game, both you and your friend will have the use of these ARC Codes to battle each other.

ARC CODE	KEY IN . . .	EFFECT . . .
1	AASSIEUT	Unrestricted ground movement
2	AAKIGAGA	Unrestricted flying movement

Archon is a trademark of Free Fall Associates and Electronic Arts.

Arkanoid™ Game

ARK Codes 1 thru 4 give you the usual life codes, including infinite lives. For a more challenging game, choose ARK Codes 11 and 12. But the best codes to check out here are definitely ARK Codes 5 thru 10—they let you megawarp direct to your favorite level! Note that using these warping codes may become a little confusing as the level number will be displayed in HEXADECIMAL!

ARK CODE	KEY IN . . .	EFFECT . . .
1	PAOPUGLA	Player 1 start with 1 life
2	TAOPUGLA	Player 1 start with 6 lives
3	PAOPUGLE	Player 1 start with 9 lives
4	OZNEATVK	Infinite lives, players 1 & 2
5	IAOONGPA	Player 1 start at level 5
6	ZAOONGPE	Player 1 start at level 10
7	YAOONGPE	Player 1 start at level 15
8	GPOONGPA	Player 1 start at level 20
9	PPOONGPE	Player 1 start at level 25
10	TPOONGPE	Player 1 start at level 30
11	SXNAIAAX	No bat enhancement capsules
12	SXVATAAX	No lasers

Pick'n'mix your codes. Try ARK Codes 1 and 12 for a more difficult game.

Arkanoid is a trademark of Taito Corporation.

Arkista's Ring™ Game

For Arkista's Ring™ we have RING Code 4 for infinite lives and RING Code 8 for infinite energy! RING Codes 5 and 6 let you start with more or fewer hearts, making the game harder or easier to suit your style. And for plenty of extra continues, check out RING Code 9.

RING CODE	KEY IN . . .	EFFECT . . .
1	PAKETILA	1 life
2	TAKETILA	6 lives
3	PAKETILE	9 lives
4	SZULXKVK	Infinite lives
5	ZAKATIIA	Start with fewer hearts
6	PAKATIIE	Start with more hearts

7	LAEPYSYA	Less damage from powerful monsters
8	GZOPTIST	Infinite energy
9	IPUAGSLA	20 continues
10	TAUAGSLA	5 continues

Arkista's Ring is a trademark of American Sammy Corp.

Astyanax™ Game

Lots of Game Genie™ codes for good 'ole Astyanax™—for a big advantage, why not pick out triple lives, a weapon power boost and the ability to keep your weapons after dying to start with? ASTY Codes 6, 9 and 10 should do the trick!

ASTY CODE	KEY IN ...	EFFECT ...
1	AUEKGUAP	Infinite spell energy
2	SZUGTISA	Infinite life energy
3	AZKAVZGO	Double life and spell energy
4	AEUEUGZA + AASAXZZA	Start with 1 life
5	IEUEUGZA + IASAXZZA	Start with double lives
6	AEUEUGZE + AASAXZZE	Start with triple lives
7	PAKEKZAA	Start with Blast Spell
8	ZAKEKZAA	Start with Bind Spell
9	GPKAXZGA	Start with extra weapon power
10	SZUGEUVK	Keep weapons after death

Remember that you can pick'n'mix your codes! You can enter up to THREE separate codes at one time, or one double-code (like ASTY Code 6) and one single code (like ASTY Code 3).

Astyanax is a trademark of Jaleco USA, Inc.
Game Genie is a trademark of Lewis Galoob Toys, Inc.

Athena™ Game

I wish I had more time, I wish I had more lives, I wish I had more energy! The Game Genie™ can grant you these three wishes and give Athena™ the power to go farther than ever before! Look down the list, pick out a few codes, then try them! On the other hand, some advanced players may want to make Athena more challenging—try ATH Codes 1 and 8 together and see how well you do!

ATH CODE	KEY IN ...	EFFECT ...
1	AEKNLPZA	Start with 1 life
2	IEKNLPZA	Start with 6 lives
3	AEKNLPZE	Start with 9 lives
4	GZUZLISA	Don't take any damage (after first 2 units)

Some codes may cause undesired effects (which are not permanent). If this occurs,

5	AXKNYOGA	Start with energy boost
6	AAULLYPA	Freeze timer
7	YASVAYIA	Start with extra time
8	GASVAYIA	Start with less time

Remember that you can pick'n'mix your codes—you can enter up to THREE separate ATH Codes at the same time.

Athena is a trademark of SNK Corp. of America.
Game Genie is a trademark of Lewis Galoob Toys, Inc.

Back to the Future™ Game

Game Genie™ is here to help get Marty™ out of the 50's and back to his own time—before it's too late! Try BACK Code 2 to start with 8 lives, or BACK Codes 3 thru 6 for extra help in some of those tricky situations. Even with the Delorean, he may get pressed for time—check out BACK Code 7 to make time stand still!

BACK
CODE   KEY IN . . .   EFFECT . . .

1	PEXEGAGA	Start with 1 life
2	AEXEGAGE	Start with 8 lives
3	SZKEGOVK	Never lose a life in Hill Valley game
4	SXOELOVK	Never lose a life in Cafe game
5	SXKALOVK	Never lose a life in School game
6	SXVELOVK	Never lose a life in Dancing Hall game
7	AVVOUZSZ	Disable all timers

Remember that you can pick'n'mix your codes. For the best effect enter THREE codes at once!

Back to the Future and Marty are trademarks of Universal City Studios Inc. Used by LJN Toys, Ltd. under license.
Game Genie is a trademark of Lewis Galoob Toys, Inc.

Back to the Future II & III™ Game

FUTURE Codes 1 and 2 give you plenty of extra lives and FUTURE Codes 4 and 5 give you extra nuclear fuel! For rapid-fire shots, check out FUTURE Code 7. And to keep your shots after losing a life or continuing, see FUTURE Code 8.

FUTURE
CODE   KEY IN . . .   EFFECT . . .

1	ZAXKZZPA	20 lives
2	LAXKZZPA	30 lives
3	SXXELOVK	Infinite lives
4	ZAXKYZPA	20 nuclear fuel units
5	LAXKYZPA	30 nuclear fuel units
6	GZEEPZST + GZOEZZST	Infinite fuel
7	PEKASEPO	Quicker shots
8	GZKAKGSA	Keep shots

Remember that you can pick'n'mix your codes.

Back to the Future II & III is a trademark of Universal City Studios Inc. Used by LJN Toys, Ltd. under license.

refer to pages 10 and 11 for instructions. If you still have problems, call 1-513-868-8835.

Bad Dudes™ Game

You've got to be bad in Bad Dudes™! If you're not bad enough then maybe you need BAD Code 5. If you're not bad at all then you badly need BAD Code 7! But seriously, if you're already quite good at Bad Dudes, then try using BAD Code 6 to give yourself a fighting chance.

BAD CODE	KEY IN . . .	EFFECT . . .	
1	SZNKASVK	Infinite lives	
2	GXOKASVK	Infinite continues	
3	PENXYZLA	Start with 1 life and 1 continue	
4	TENXYZLA	Start with double lives and continues	
5	PENXYZLE	Start with triple lives and continues	
6	PESAIYIE	Gain double usual energy from drinks	
7	APEETPEY	Become completely invincible!	

Remember that you can pick'n'mix your codes! You can enter up to THREE Game Genie™ codes at one time.

Bad Dudes is a trademark of Data East USA, Inc.
Game Genie is a trademark of Lewis Galoob Toys, Inc.

Bad Street Brawler™ Game

It's a real zoo out there—if you want to nail those no-gooders properly, here's a few Game Genie™ codes that let you do just that! BRAW Code 1 is the obvious choice if you want to explore the whole game. Why not try one of the level warp codes (BRAW Codes 5 thru 7) instead?

BRAW CODE	KEY IN . . .	EFFECT . . .	
1	OZOIYPVK	Infinite lives	
2	PAXITALA	Start with 1 life	
3	TAXITALA	Start with 6 lives	
4	PAXITALE	Start with 9 lives	
5	GEUZZYAA	Start on level 5	
6	PEUZZYAE	Start on level 10	
7	TEUZZYAE	Start on level 15	
8	YENIZNZE	Increase energy	
9	SZOITNVK	Don't die at time out	

Remember that you can pick'n'mix your codes! You can enter up to THREE different BRAW Codes at one time.

Bad Street Brawler is a trademark of Mattel, Inc.
Game Genie is a trademark of Lewis Galoob Toys, Inc.

Balloon Fight™ Game

Here's a few codes to enhance this brilliantly playable game. As well as the usual infinite lives code, we also have a handful of level warps, and a couple of more interesting codes (check out LOON Codes 5 and 6).

LOON CODE	KEY IN . . .	EFFECT . . .	
1	SUNNIZVI	Infinite lives	

Some codes may cause undesired effects (which are not permanent). If this occurs,

2	AENYPPZA	Start with 1 life
3	IENYPPZA	Start with 6 lives
4	AENYPPZE	Start with 9 lives
5	PEUYTLZA	Start with only one balloon
6	AVXTNYKA	Balloons are unburstable
7	GENNIPAA	Start on level 5—2 players only
8	PENNIPAE	Start on level 10—2 players only
9	TENNIPAE	Start on level 15—2 players only

Balloon Fight is a trademark of Nintendo of America Inc.

Batman™ Game

For Batman™ you get all the regular Game Genie™ codes to change the number of lives (and you thought he was invincible!), as well as some more interesting ones. You can use BAT Code 5 to make picking up the hearts really worthwhile . . . and if you call yourself a REAL game player, try using BAT Codes 2 and 8 together—good luck!

BAT CODE	KEY IN . . .	EFFECT . . .
1	SZUGGTVG	Infinite lives
2	AEESKGZA	Start with 1 life
3	IEESKGZA	Start with 6 lives
4	AEESKGZE	Start with 9 lives
5	GEEPOTPA	Extra energy on heart pick-up
6	GZNOUGST	Infinite pellets after pick-up
7	GPSPXVZA	Double usual pellets on pick-up
8	IASPXVZA	Half usual pellets on pick-up

Remember that you can pick'n'mix your codes—you can enter up to THREE separate BAT Codes at the same time.

Batman is a trademark of DC Comics Inc. Used by Sun Corporation of America under license.
Game Genie is a trademark of Lewis Galoob Toys, Inc.

Battle of Olympus™ Game

You can try some interesting codes here. OLY Code 1 will make the game more difficult, and OLY Codes 2 thru 7 will give you an advantage.

OLY CODE	KEY IN . . .	EFFECT . . .
1	AAUGPAAO	Start with less stamina
2	AZUGPAAP	Start with more stamina
3	GXSSNASA	Keep stamina
4	PAUGYAAA + GZUKGASA + GZUKTASA	Start with Staff of Fennel™
5	ZAUGYAAA + GZUKGASA + GZUKTASA	Start with Sword
6	LAUGYAAA + GZUKGASA + GZUKTASA	Start with Divine Sword™
7	AAEGOZZA	Start with Sandals of Hermes™

refer to pages 10 and 11 for instructions. If you still have problems, call 1-513-868-8835.

29

Remember that you can pick'n'mix your codes! You can enter up to THREE single codes at one time, or one triple-code (like OLY Code 4).

Battle of Olympus, Staff of Fennel, Divine Sword and Sandals of Hermes are trademarks of Broderbund Software Inc.

Bigfoot™ Game

Ever wanted the really best engine, but just couldn't afford it? Well FOOT Code 5 makes engines half price! With FOOT Codes 5 thru 12 you can change the price of all the car parts. If two of you are playing and you're not quite evenly matched, FOOT Code 2 gives player 1 a big advantage—he or she gets all of players 2's nitros!

FOOT
CODE	KEY IN ...	EFFECT ...	
1	SUKXVUVS	Infinite nitros	
2	VTVUYOVN + SZVUAOSE	Player 1 gets player 2's nitros	⚡
3	NNKXXLGV	Longer nitro boost	
4	AXKXXLGT	Shorter nitro boost	⚡
5	GEKAOKAA	Engines are half price	
6	PEKAOKAE	Engines cost more	
7	LEKAXGTA	Tires are half price	
8	PEKAXGTE	Tires cost more	💰
9	ZEKAUGGA	Transmission work is half price	
10	AEKAUGGE	Transmission work is double price	
11	PEKAKGZA	Suspension is half price	
12	TEKAKGZA	Suspension is triple price	

Remember that you can pick'n'mix your codes. You can enter up to THREE separate codes at one time.

Bigfoot is a trademark of Acclaim Entertainment, Inc.

Bionic Commando™ Game

Bionic Commando™ is an excellent game! You can start the game with your 3-way gun if you use BIO Code 6, and then you can use BIO Code 11 for an autofire feature!

BIO
CODE	KEY IN ...	EFFECT ...	
1	SZNUIYVG	Infinite lives in main game	🎰
2	SXUEZPVG	Infinite lives in sub-game	
3	AAUGSZZA	Start with 1 life	
4	IAUGSZZA	Start with double lives	👪
5	AAUGSZZE	Start with triple lives	
6	VGKKNXUK	Start with 3-way gun	🔫
7	LAUKOZAA + XTUKUXVU	Start with 3 life energy capsules	🎴
8	SXSTYNVK	Don't take damage from bullets and collisions	
9	VTNZXVVK	Don't take damage from spikes	🚫
10	SZUOAOVK	Don't take damage from bullets and collisions in sub-game	

    Some codes may cause undesired effects (which are not permanent). If this occurs,

| 11 | XYXUUOEN | Autofire—main game |
| 12 | AAKUOOZA | Use with BIO Code 11 for improved autofire with normal gun |

Remember that you can pick'n'mix your codes! You could try using BIO Codes 11 and 12 together to give brilliant autofire with your normal gun.

Bionic Commando is a trademark of Capcom USA, Inc.

Blades of Steel™ Game

Try STEEL Code 1—faster timer—and you'll have one frantic game on your hands! And for the best chance of winning fights, be sure to check out STEEL Code 3—it limits you to one punch each, and you always get to punch first!

STEEL CODE	KEY IN ...	EFFECT ...
1	GEUGTTYA	Faster timer
2	GOUGTTYA	Slower timer
3	PAXZLGIA	Players can take only one punch
4	AAOSSAAZ	Player with puck doesn't slow down

Remember that you can pick'n'mix your codes.

Blades of Steel is a trademark of Konami Inc.

Blaster Master™ Game

These Game Genie™ codes can help you beat the monsters in the sewers! As you know, you normally start off with no weapons at all, but using MAST Codes 8 thru 10 you can alter the game to start off with a selectable number of each special weapon.

MAST CODE	KEY IN ...	EFFECT ...
1	SZUGYIVG	Infinite lives
2	AAEGZLZA	Start with 1 life
3	IAEGZLZA	Start with 6 lives
4	AAEGZLZE	Start with 9 lives
5	GZSOEEVK	Infinite homing missiles
6	GXKPEOVK	Infinite Thunderbreaks™
7	GXSOVXVK	Infinite multi-warheads
8	IAEKPLAA	Start with 5 of each weapon
9	ZAEKPLAE	Start with 10 of each weapon
10	YAEKPLA	Start with 15 of each weapon

Remember that you can pick'n'mix your codes! You can enter up to THREE different MAST Codes at one time.

Blaster Master and Thunderbreaks are trademarks of Sun Corporation of America.
Game Genie is a trademark of Lewis Galoob Toys, Inc.

Bomberman™ Game

Here's a fistful of excellent codes for Bomberman™ fans! Be sure to check out BOMB Code 4, which stops the timer. You'll also get extra blasting power with BOMB Codes 12 thru 14, extra time to get out of the way of exploding bombs with BOMB Code 15, or you can play 'chicken' and reduce your escape time with BOMB Code 16. You can also have a 'Demo Start', or become immune to blasts or even walk through walls. Just take your pick!

BOMB CODE	KEY IN...	EFFECT...	
1	SXPKAG	Infinite lives	
2	AEZKLL	Start with 1 life	
3	PEZKLU	Start with 10 lives	
4	SZIGAT	Stop timer	
5	VPGKGG	Decrease time	
6	VYGKGK	Increase timer	
7	ZELGYU	Start on stage 10	
8	GOLGYL	Start on stage 20	
9	TOLGYU	Start on stage 30	
10	AXLGYU	Start on stage 40	
11	ZULGYL	Start on stage 50	
12	AXKKALAP	Start with double power bomb blasts	
13	AUKKALAP	Start with triple power bomb blasts	
14	EEKKALAP	Start with maximum power bomb blasts!	
15	NYXKUIEX	Increase bomb detonation time	
16	AYXKUIEZ	Reduce bomb detonation time	
17	XZEGNIVZ + PAEKEIGN	Use up to 9 bombs	
18	OXEKVPSX + AESKNKTA	Start with and keep remote controller	
19	GXEKLGSA	Never lose remote controller after pick-up	
20	AESKGUIZ	Demo start—start with remote controller, bigger bombs and more bombsboy	
21	OXVGITSX	Immune to bomb blasts	
22	OZNKNNPK + AEEGEYPA	Walk through walls	

Remember that you can pick'n'mix your codes. BOMB Codes 3 and 10 are a good combination to try!

Bomberman is a trademark of Hudson Soft USA, Inc.

Some codes may cause undesired effects (which are not permanent). If this occurs,

Boulderdash™ Game

DASH Code 3 gives you extra lives and DASH Code 9 extends the time you have to complete each level. But remember that the quicker you finish, the higher you score! DASH Code 8, on the other hand, gives you a lot LESS time to finish—a challenge to any Boulderdash™ player!

DASH CODE	KEY IN...	EFFECT...	
1	SLEZXTVI	Infinite lives	
2	PAKIELLA	1 life	
3	TAKIELLA	6 lives	
4	PAKIELLE	9 lives	
5	PEOXEYLA	1 life after continue	
6	TEOXEYLA	6 lives after continue	
7	PEOXEYLE	9 lives after continue	
8	YOSGXNYU	Speed up timer	
9	NNSGXNYU	Slow down timer	
10	SXSGSYAX	Stop timer	

Remember that you can pick'n'mix your codes. You can enter up to THREE separate codes at one time.

Boulderdash is a trademark of First Star, Inc. Used by Data East Corporation under license.

A Boy and His Blob™ Game

Having trouble with your Blob™? A few more jellybeans (BLOB Code 4) would probably come in handy. You can also change the game in a 'bigger' way—you can become indestructible with BLOB Code 7, or experience the 'Fast Play' mode with BLOB Code 6.

NOTE FOR BLOB CODE 7: In the underwater section, if you lose a life you may not be able to call your Blob, and therefore become trapped. If this happens, just reset and start again.

BLOB CODE	KEY IN...	EFFECT...	
1	AAULNGIA	1 life only	
2	ZAULNGIE	Double lives	
3	GXXEOPVG	Infinite lives	
4	SZXLXKSU + YYXLUGEY	Gives 101 of all starting Jellybeans	
5	AAVKIPPA	Infinite Jellybeans	
6	SXEEZAAX	Fast play	
7	AVOGAEOZ	Invincible	
8	AVOPVGEI	Never take damage from enemies	
9	APEUUIAA	Gives 10 Orange Jellybeans	
10	AONUSGAA	10 Lime Jellybeans	
11	OONLOGZN	99 Licorice Jellybeans	

refer to pages 10 and 11 for instructions. If you still have problems, call 1-513-868-8835.

12	AUNLUGIP	Double Strawberry Jellybeans	
13	TUNLNKAP	Double Cola Jellybeans	
14	AKNUOGGX	Double Cinnamon Jellybeans	
15	GXNUUGZP	Double Apple Jellybeans	
16	AVNUNGAL	Double Vanilla Jellybeans	
17	ZPELNITA	Double Ketchup Jellybeans	
18	AONLSGTE	Triple Coconut Jellybeans	
19	APELUITE	Triple Rootbeer Jellybeans	
20	APEUSIAA	10 Vitamin A for Vita-Blaster™	
21	APEUNIAA	10 Vitamin B for Vita-Blaster	
22	APOLOIAA	10 Vitamin C for Vita-Blaster	

Remember, you can program your own codes! BLOB Codes 9, 10 and 11 through 22 might make good codes to try your programming luck on!

A Boy and His Blob, Blob and Vita-Blaster are trademarks of Absolute Entertainment, Inc.

Breakthru™ Game

If you're a Breakthru™ expert, but your friend isn't, then why not use THRU Code 3 to give yourself 1 life, and THRU Code 8 to give 9 lives to player 2. That should even things out nicely . . . and, of course, you could use THRU Code 13 at the same time to get things going with a bang!

THRU CODE	KEY IN . . .	EFFECT . . .	
1	GZUKYPVG	Infinite lives for both players	
2	GZKSLZVG	Freeze weapon timer	
3	PEUKPZLA	Player 1 start with 1 life	
4	PEKGGZLA	Player 2 start with 1 life	
5	TEUKPZLA	Player 1 start with 6 lives	
6	TEKGGZLA	Player 2 start with 6 lives	
7	PEUKPZLE	Player 1 start with 9 lives	
8	PEKGGZLE	Player 2 start with 9 lives	
9	ZANKLZPA	Start game on level 2	
10	LANKLZPA	Start game on level 3	
11	GANKLZPA	Start game on level 4	
12	IANKLZPA	Start game on level 5	
13	LTUKTLAA	Start each life with 3-way firing and 99 seconds	

Remember that you can pick'n'mix your codes! You can enter up to THREE different THRU Codes at one time.

Breakthru is a trademark of Data East USA, Inc.

Bubble Bobble™ Game

Have you ever wondered what the later levels in this brilliant bubble-blowing bonanza look like? Now you're free to investigate as far as you can, with a few extra lives and a warp to a higher level! Try BUB Code 3 and BUB Code 7 together to see what we mean. BUB Code 13 will

34

Some codes may cause undesired effects (which are not permanent). If this occurs,

boost your bubble power and BUB Code 14 lets you zoom thru the levels with a handy pair of turbo shoes!

BUB CODE	KEY IN . . .	EFFECT . . .	
1	PAUKEZLA	Both players start with 1 life	
2	TAUKEZLA	Both players start with 6 lives	
3	PAUKEZLE	Both players start with 9 lives	
4	ZAUGEZPE	Start game on level 10	
5	PPUGEZPE	Start game on level 25	
6	ZLUGEZPA	Start game on level 50	
7	LGUGEZPE	Start game on level 75	
8	ZAOGOLGA	Skip only 2 levels	
9	ZAOGOLGE	Skip 10 levels	
10	ZANEAGPA + NNEEAKVN	Monsters move faster	
11	LANEAGPA + NNEEAKSN	Monsters move super fast	
12	LANEIGZA + SNEEIKVN	Angry monsters move faster	
13	AAUILSPP	Lots of bubble power	
14	AANSIGTA + AESIPGTA	Always wear turbo shoes	

Remember that you can pick 'n' mix your codes!
Bubble Bobble is a trademark of Taito America Corporation

The Bugs Bunny™ Birthday Blow Out™ Game

To help Bugs™ make it to his birthday party, why not try out some of these great codes? BUGS Code 1 gives you infinite lives. BUGS Code 2 gives you mega-jump, which really helps when you're trying to reach those carrots. And BUGS Code 3 boosts your energy when you find hearts.

BUGS CODE	KEY IN. . .	EFFECT. . .	
1	SZVIGKVK	Infinite lives	
2	LAOANZTE	Mega-jumping Bugs	
3	AEOXPZGE	Two hearts of energy gained on pick-up	
4	PEOXPZGA	Less energy gained on pick-up	
5	ATNZALAL	Stunned for longer	
6	IPNZALAL	Stunned for less time	
7	AASAKOTL	Use hammer when stunned	

Remember that you can pick'n'mix your codes. You can enter up to THREE separate codes at one time.
Bugs Bunny and Bugs are trademarks of Warner Bros.Inc.

Bugs Bunny™—The Bugs Bunny Crazy Castle™ Game

As well as the usual infinite lives and level warps, we've got a really ace code (BUGS Code 5) that'll make gamers the world over very grateful—check it out! But if you've already beaten the game, then try BUGS Codes 6 and 7—they'll make it much more challenging.

BUGS
CODE	KEY IN . . .	EFFECT . . .	
1	SZOKGPVG	Start with infinite lives	
2	PAUGPAIA	Start with 1 life	
3	ZAUGPAIE	Start with 10 lives	
4	PXXTGGEN + PXXTAGAO	Start with super rabbit punches	
5	GXETZZEI	Become invincible	
6	GXKGZZEY	Baddies go as fast as Bugs Bunny™	
7	GASGAAPA	Make platforms invisible!	
8	SZOKGAAX + PEXYVYAE	Start on level 10	
9	SZOKGAAX + LOXYVYAA	Start on level 20	
10	SZOKGAAX + IOXYVYAE	Start on level 30	
11	SZOKGAAX + YXXYVYAA	Start on level 40	

Remember that you can pick'n'mix your codes! You can enter up to THREE separate codes at one time, or one double-code (like BUGS Code 4) and one single code (like BUGS Code 2).
Bugs Bunny and The Bugs Bunny Crazy Castle are trademarks of Warner Bros. Inc. Used by Kemco Seika Corp. under license

Bump'n'Jump™ Game
You can completely change the playability of Bump'n'Jump™ with these codes. With BUMP Code 1, you'll always be able to jump, and if you combine it with BUMP Code 3, you can jump no matter what speed you're going, too!

BUMP
CODE	KEY IN . . .	EFFECT . . .	
1	AAVPNLGP	Jump OK, even with no power	
2	ZAUZAIPA	Gain double power on every pick-up	
3	AGVONLAA	Jump OK at any speed	
4	PANPNLIE	Set jump OK speed to 190	
5	LANPNLIA	Set jump OK speed to 130	
6	GEOAGGAA	Start on scene 5	
7	PEOAGGAE	Start on scene 10	
8	TEOAGGAE	Start on scene 15	

Remember that you can pick'n'mix your codes! You can enter up to THREE different BUMP Codes at one time.
Bump'n'Jump is a trademark of Data East USA, Inc.

Burai Fighter™ Game
BURA Codes 1 thru 3 give you a whole load of extra lives. If that's not enough, BURA Code 4 gives you infinite lives on ALL levels! To give your weapons a power boost, try BURA Codes 5 thru 7. And if you want to keep hold of ALL your fighting aids, including weapons, speed ups and rotating pods, be sure to check out BURA Code 14—it's the best!

Some codes may cause undesired effects (which are not permanent). If this occurs,

B

BURA
CODE	KEY IN . . .	EFFECT . . .
1	PEOLATIE	Extra lives for Eagle level
2	AEOLPTGE	Extra lives for Albatross level
3	TEOLZTLA	Extra lives for Ace level
4	VNOTENVK	Infinite lives
5	LAXTTPPA	More power for weapons
6	ZAXTTPPE	Maximum power for weapons
7	PASVTPZE	Increase cobalt power picked up
8	VTVNIPSA	Start with laser
9	VTNYPPSA	Start with rotating pod
10	OUVNAXOO	Never lose weapon power
11	KXNYLZSA	Never lose speed up
12	KXVNYZSA	Never lose weapons
13	KXNYPZSA	Never lose rotating pod
14	AVVNLXOZ	Never lose ANYTHING!

Remember that you can pick'n'mix your codes. You can enter up to THREE separate codes at one time.
Burai Fighter is a trademark of Taxan USA Corp.

BurgerTime™ Game

BURG Code 5 is a clever one—Peter Pepper™ gets a shiny new pair of anti-gravity shoes! As well as platforms and ladders, your little chef will be able to walk on thin air! For the BurgerTime™ experts out there in gaming land, we have a Game Genie™ code to make things move a little faster—BURG Code 7.

BURG
CODE	KEY IN . . .	EFFECT . . .
1	SZSTVAVI	Start game with infinite lives
2	AASGKLGE	Start game with 8 lives
3	SLKIZYVI	Start game with infinite peppers
4	APVGSLIA	Start game with double peppers
5	GZVIAZEI	Anti-gravity shoes
6	YPESOUGO	Peter Pepper gets super speed
7	SZKNNIAX	Fast play for experts
8	SXVSSXSU	Monsters always move slowly
9	SXVSSXSU + GOVSVXAO	Monsters move at double speed
10	SXVSSXSU + YOVSVXAO	Monsters move at quadruple speed

Remember that you can pick'n'mix your codes! You can enter up to THREE separate codes at one time, or one double-code (like BURG Code 10) and one single code (like BURG Code 6).
BurgerTime and Peter Pepper are trademarks of Data East USA, Inc.
Game Genie is a trademark of Lewis Galoob Toys, Inc.

---

refer to pages 10 and 11 for instructions. If you still have problems, call 1-513-868-8835.

Cabal™ Game

Blast your way thru Cabal™ with your choice of lives, grenades and immunity time. You can go for a really tough game with CAB Codes 2, 8 and 9, or else you could combine CAB Codes 3, 6 and 10, and the enemy won't stand a chance!

CAB CODE	KEY IN . . .	EFFECT . . .	
1	UNUOTTNN	9 lives for players 1 and 2	
2	UNUOTTNY	1 life for players 1 and 2	
3	GXEOZZVI	Infinite lives	
4	KYVEOZUY	Start with 20 grenades	
5	NYVEOZUY	Start with 50 grenades	
6	AEUXSIPA	Infinite grenades	
7	GAVXNGGE	Pick up more grenades	
8	ZAVXNGGA	Pick up less grenades	
9	AKOPLZEG	Shorter immunity	
10	NNOPLLEK	Longer immunity	

Remember that you can pick'n'mix your codes. Enter up to THREE separate codes at one time.
Cabal is a trademark of Fabtek, Inc.

Captain Skyhawk™ Game

Here are some excellent Game Genie™ codes! HAWK Codes 7 thru 9 let you adjust your missile armament to make the game easier or harder. HAWK Code 4 gives you extra lives, bombs and credits. HAWK Codes 10 thru 12 can make the game more difficult by doubling the cost of the missiles; you'll still see the original price on the screen, but you'll have to pay more!

HAWK CODE	KEY IN . . .	EFFECT . . .	
1	OZKAIGVK	Infinite lives	
2	PEUITIIA	Start with 1 life	
3	ZEUITIIE	Start with 10 lives	
4	AEVIGITP	Mega start	
5	OZXPUZVK	Infinite Maverick missiles	
6	OXKPVGVK	Infinite Hawk bombs	
7	LESITITA	Start with half Hawk bombs	
8	GOSITITA	Start with 20 Hawk bombs	
9	AESSZIZE	Start with 8 Phoenix and Maverick missiles	
10	GENXKGZA	Double cost of Hawk bombs	
11	GAXZKIZA	Double cost of Phoenix missiles	
12	ZAOZEIIE	Double cost of Maverick missiles	

Remember that you can pick'n'mix your codes. Enter up to THREE separate codes at one time.
Captain Skyhawk is a trademark of Milton Bradley Company.
Game Genie is a trademark of Lewis Galoob Toys, Inc.

Some codes may cause undesired effects (which are not permanent). If this occurs,

Castle of Dragon™ Game

Get off to a mega start with CAST Code 10 for super fighting power! Use CAST Code 2 to make the action a bit more frantic, or use CAST Code 1 to put those scary skeletons in a good mood for a change! Have fun.

CAST CODE	KEY IN . . .	EFFECT . . .
1	PEVPULAP	Stop skeletons from fighting
2	GEOGYZPA	Enemies and you each fight faster!
3	ZPSLONLP	Super strong monsters
4	SZVUSNVK	No harm from most monster attacks
5	YNOLSYAE	Infinite energy
6	NYXKLAGE	Super energy
7	ZAXGLAAA	Start with knives
8	LAXGLAAA	Start with knives and mace
9	EAXGLAAA	Start with armor
10	UAXGLAAA	Start with armor, knives and mace!

Castle of Dragon is a trademark of Seta, USA, Inc.

CastleQuest™ Game

Among the many Game Genie™ codes for CastleQuest™, we have some that will give you extra lives and better swordsmanship. QEST Code 8 can't be used alone—it must be used in conjunction with QEST Code 7, and will give you a brilliant permanent sword-wielding ability!

QEST CODE	KEY IN . . .	EFFECT . . .
1	SXKAVIVG	Infinite lives
2	ATSXATEY	Infinite keys
3	LKUZTZZU	75 lives instead of 50
4	POUZTZZU	25 lives instead of 50
5	SXKNKLVG	Don't lose life from 'reset' or 'back' options
6	SZOEIUVK	Use sword (press 'B') as long as you like
7	XXOAZGYA	Now you can move while using sword . . .
8	IAEEALYP	Must use with Code 7 for permanent sword-wielding ability!
9	GAXEGIZA + GAUEGIZA	Supercharged speed-up
10	AAXEGIZE + AAUEGIZE	Turbo fuel-injected 16-valve speed-up

Remember that you can pick'n'mix your codes! You can enter up to THREE separate codes at one time, or one double-code (like QEST Code 9) and one single code (like QEST Code 1).

CastleQuest is a trademark of Nexoft Corporation.
Game Genie is a trademark of Lewis Galoob Toys, Inc.

CastleVania™ Game

Wouldn't CastleVania™ be a little easier if you had all the time in the world? Well CAS Code 7 will give you just that. In the meantime, CAS Code 8 lets you hang on to your weapons after you've lost a life, and CAS Code 9 gives you rapid firepower. Why not have some friends over for a CastleVania exploring party?

NOTE: You may notice some extra flicker on the screen. Try pressing the RESET button to clear it.

CAS CODE	KEY IN . . .	EFFECT . . .	
1	OXNGLZVK	Infinite lives	
2	KZSSEZKA + KXESUZKA	Weapons don't use power hearts	
3	PANKXPGA + PANGSAGA	Start with 1 life	
4	AANKXPGE + AANGSAGE	Start with 8 lives	
5	AXOGOPIE	Start with 40 power hearts	
6	ASOGOPIA	Start with 80 power hearts	
7	SXXXYAAX	Infinite time	
8	GZOGYUSE	Keep weapons after losing a life	
9	ZEUTAYAA	Gain rapid fire shots on weapon pick-up	

Remember that you can pick'n'mix your codes! You can enter up to THREE separate codes at one time, or one double-code (like CAS Code 4) and one single code (like CAS Code 5).
CastleVania is a trademark of Konami Inc.

CastleVania™ II: Simon's Quest™ Game

Some gamers will have finished this game—for them we have a couple of Game Genie™ gems to make Simon's Quest™ harder; VAN Code 2 gives you only 1 life, while VAN Code 8 gives you less energy to play with. The rest of you should look at VAN Code 1, which is no doubt just what you wanted!

VAN CODE	KEY IN . . .	EFFECT . . .	
1	SZSSYLSA	Infinite energy	
2	PASGLILA	Start with 1 life	
3	TASGLILA	Start with 6 lives	
4	PASGLILE	Start with 9 lives	
5	IZSKZIAI	Start game with 25 hearts	
6	IYSKZIAI	Start game with 75 hearts	
7	AISKTIAL	Start with more energy	
8	AZSKTIAL	Start with less energy	

Remember you can program your own codes! VAN Codes 5 and 6 might make good codes to try your programming luck on!
CastleVania and Simon's Quest are trademarks of Konami Inc.
Game Genie is a trademark of Lewis Galoob Toys, Inc.

Some codes may cause undesired effects (which are not permanent). If this occurs,

Chip 'N Dale™ Game

Here's a selection of handy codes for those lovable little detectives! If you want to keep those nasty bulldogs at bay, check out CHIP Code 2. Also try CHIP Code 10—mega-jump—and whiz right over anything that's in your way!

NOTE: DON'T USE THE INVINCIBILITY CODE WITH ANY OF THE FREEZE CODES, 'CAUSE YOU MAY GET 'STUCK.' IF YOU DO, JUST PRESS RESET AND START AGAIN.

CHIP CODE	KEY IN . . .	EFFECT . . .	
1	YAKAYEPA	Invincibility (DO NOT use with Codes 2 thru 9!)	
2	ATUEENSL	Freeze mechanical bulldog	
3	AVKAVNSL	Freeze mechanical mice	
4	AVOPTESL	Freeze buzzer	
5	AVNOLKSL	Freeze buzz bomb	
6	AVVPZSSL	Freeze racket-rod	
7	ATSOYKSL	Freeze ditz	
8	ATSPANSL	Freeze hawk bomber	
9	AVVOOUSL	Freeze bouncing boxes	
10	ZEXKNPTE	Mega-jump	

Remember that you can pick'n'mix your codes. You can enter up to THREE codes at one time!

Chip 'N Dale is a trademark of The Walt Disney Company.

Chubby Cherub™ Game

Sweet little Chubby Cherub™ could do with infinite power—CHER Code 2 gives him just that! You can also shoot your bow as many times as you like if you use CHER Code 11 . . .keep right on flying and find those kids!

CHER CODE	KEY IN . . .	EFFECT . . .	
1	SZEAYZVG	Infinite lives	
2	SZEXIYSA	Infinite power	
3	AEOAAZZA	Start with 1 life	
4	IEOAAZZA	Start with double lives	
5	AEOAAZZE	Start with triple lives	
6	IEOALZPA + GEOAPZAA	Start on Stage 5	
7	ZEOALZPE + PEOAPZAE	Start on Stage 10	
8	GEVAKVAA	Half regular power gained from food	
9	PENXATZA	Slow down power loss on the ground	
10	LENXTVPA	Slow down power loss in the air	
11	ZANEVSUT	Infinite Gau™ (shots)	
12	AASXOAGE	Double Gau (shots) on candy pick-up	

Remember that you can pick'n'mix your codes! You can enter up to THREE separate codes at one time, or one double-code (like CHER Code 7) and one other code (like CHER Code 11).
Chubby Cherub and Gau are trademarks of Bandai America, Inc.

Circus Caper™ Game

CAPE Code 2 boosts your energy back up to full whenever you find food. This comes in very handy, especially on the harder levels. CAPE Code 3 starts you off with a whole host of great weapons and CAPE Codes 5 thru 9 let you start on any level!

CAPE CODE	KEY IN . . .	EFFECT . . .	
1	GZEYPSSE	Infinite energy	
2	AASVNAZA	Full energy from food	
3	NNOTNLAE	Start with lots of weapons	
4	SUNVOKVS	Infinite weapons	
5	ZEVGGAPA	Start on stage 2	
6	LEVGGAPA	Start on stage 3	
7	GEVGGAPA	Start on stage 4	
8	IEVGGAPA	Start on stage 5	
9	TEVGGAPA	Start on stage 6	

Remember that you can pick'n'mix your codes. You can enter up to THREE separate codes at one time.
Circus Caper is a trademark of Toho Co., Ltd.

City Connection™ Game

Vroom! Vroom! Tokyo, here we come! If you find this game too hard, then here's 10 Game Genie™ codes to help. Don't forget that you can enter up to THREE codes in any order—they'll still work!

CITY CODE	KEY IN . . .	EFFECT . . .	
1	SZNSTPVG	Infinite lives	
2	IEKEYIZA	Start with double lives	
3	AEKEYIZE	Start with triple lives	
4	SXKPZGVG	Infinite oil	
5	AXSAPIIA	Start with extra oil	
6	PEKEIIAA	Start on level 1	
7	ZEKEIIAA	Start on level 2	
8	LEKEIIAA	Start on level 3	
9	GEKEIIAA	Start on level 4	
10	IEKEIIAA	Start on level 5	

Remember that you can pick'n'mix your codes—you can enter up to THREE separate codes into your Game Genie™ at one time!
City Connection is a trademark of Jaleco USA Inc.
Game Genie is a trademark of Lewis Galoob Toys, Inc.

Some codes may cause undesired effects (which are not permanent). If this occurs,

Clash at Demonhead™ Game

An interesting Game Genie™ code is HEAD Code 6, which arranges things so that once you have bought an item in the super shop, you have an infinite supply of them. Also, look at HEAD Code 7, which causes the shopkeeper to give out freebies! Try just making things a little easier before you leap in by using HEAD Code 1.

HEAD CODE	KEY IN . . .	EFFECT . . .	
1	VZSULOVV	Don't die when power hits zero	
2	VNNGNUSO	Start with 1 of each item	
3	AAEKVGAO + AEVZNPAO + ZAOGXGGA	Start with 50% power	
4	APEKVGAO + TAOGXGGA + AOVZNPAO	Start with 150% power	
5	AZEKVGAP + AAOGXGGE + AXVZNPAP	Start with 200% power	
6	SXKZGSVS	Infinite supply of all items bought	
7	AVUGAGST	All items in shop are free	
8	TAUGKGKY + UPUGVKXO	Start with extra cash!	

Remember that you can pick'n'mix your codes, but not if you are using HEAD Code 3 thru 5—they each use up the whole Game Genie™ code screen.

Clash at Demonhead is a trademark of Vic Tokai, Inc.
Game Genie is a trademark of Lewis Galoob Toys, Inc.

Clu Clu Land™ Game

Clu Clu Land™ can be radically easier by using either CLU Code 1 OR CLU Code 2. But using both would be silly—even a sleeping hedgehog in a wet paper bag could play well using both the codes at the same time! On the other hand, CLU Code 8 makes the game harder by making your rays a lot shorter—you'll have to engage the enemy at close quarters!

CLU CODE	KEY IN . . .	EFFECT . . .	
1	GXLILL	Both players have infinite lives	
2	GZPGSL	Infinite time (stops timer)	
3	PAGKGL	Both players start with 1 life	
4	APGKGL	Both players start with 10 lives	
5	TEYIGL	Increase extra time	
6	VTSKPLSA	Player 2 has only 1 life	
7	IEVISZZA	Shoot more rays	
8	AOVSOZAZ	Shoot shorter rays	
9	ASVSOZAZ	Shoot longer rays	
10	AASIAYGA	Enemy can go thru gold bars	

Remember that you can pick'n'mix your codes!

Clu Clu Land is a trademark of Nintendo of America Inc.

Cobra Command™ Game

We've been tweaking the most advanced Cobra attack helicopter ever built, and we've found that you only have to enter one Game Genie™ code (COCO Code 4) to make it completely immune to damage! The enemy can throw as much heavy weaponry as they like at it, but it won't take any
hits . . . wonder if the USAF is interested?

COCO CODE	KEY IN . . .	EFFECT . . .	
1	SXUAAOVK	Start with infinite lives	
2	AAUVGZGA	Start with 1 life	
3	AAUVGZGE	Start with 9 lives	
4	GZSSNGST	Become immune to weapon damage	

Remember that you can pick'n'mix your codes! Up to THREE separate codes can be entered at one time (but only two will be needed for this game at max).
Cobra Command is a trademark of Data East USA, Inc.
Game Genie is a trademark of Lewis Galoob Toys, Inc.

Cobra Triangle™ Game

Yippee! A real favorite . . . lots of brilliantly tricky challenges to complete within strict time limits. TRI Code 2 is great because you can just carry on playing Cobra Triangle™ all night with infinite continues! There's also TRI Code 1 to make sure you never lose your power-ups between lives. Must go now—just gotta have one more try . . .

TRI CODE	KEY IN . . .	EFFECT . . .	
1	ENXTPVSA + LEXTZVAX	Never lose your power-ups	
2	SZUXZVVK	Infinite continue options	
3	SZEVNOVK	Don't lose life for damage	
4	SZVTSOVK	Don't lose life for Time Out	
5	VVXEAUSE + LOXEPLIP	Gain an extra minute	
6	SZEVNOVK + SZVTSOVK	Infinite lives	

Remember that you can pick'n'mix your codes! You can enter up to THREE separate codes at one time, or one double-code (like TRI Code 5) and one single code (like TRI Code 4).
Cobra Triangle is a trademark of Rare, Ltd.

Code Name: Viper™ Game

You can change the number of lives with VIPE Codes 1 thru 4. (You may be able to guess what the VIPE Code for 14 lives is from this—look carefully!) You can change your firepower—and that's what the game is all about—with VIPE Codes 6 thru 14. VIPE Code 15 allows you to jump straight to the upper level without the delay of stopping and pressing UP—this could give you the edge.

VIPE CODE	KEY IN . . .	EFFECT . . .	
1	SZOVKNVK	Infinite lives	
2	PENTAGLA	Start with 1 life	
3	TENTAGLA	Start with 6 lives	
4	PENTAGLE	Start with 9 lives	

Some codes may cause undesired effects (which are not permanent). If this occurs,

5	STVPVOON + AASOVZPA	Infinite energy
6	GTETLIZL	Start with double usual bullets
7	PPETLIZU	Start with half usual bullets
8	GTOVEYZL	Double usual bullets on new life
9	PPOVEYZU	Half bullets on new life
10	VVNVGKSE	Start with machine gun and 256 bullets
11	VTOTONSE	Machine gun and 256 bullets on new life
12	GZOTONSE + GZEVVNSE	Keep machine gun after dying
13	AAOXLZPA	Infinite machine gun bullets
14	AENXZPPA	Infinite bullets for your gun
15	SXKEVNOU + ONEOYEXN	Upper level jump

Remember that you can pick'n'mix your codes! You can enter up to THREE separate codes at one time, or one double-code (like VIPE Code 15) and one other code (like VIPE Code 13).
Code Name: Viper is a trademark of Capcom USA, Inc.

Commando™ Game

Have you ever wished that Super Joe's™ hand grenades were unlimited? Well, COM Code 2 sees to that—you'll never have trouble with the gates again. If that makes it too easy for you, try instead COM Code 6, which gives you double the usual amount of grenades when you start a game—that should be all the head start you need.

COM CODE	KEY IN . . .	EFFECT . . .
1	EZEGNOVG	Start with infinite lives
2	XVULASXK	Start with infinite grenades
3	AEKKIILA	Both players start with 1 life
4	TEKKIILA	Both players start with 6 lives
5	PEKKIILE	Both players start with 9 lives
6	AOSGIIIA	Start with double rations of grenades

Remember that you can pick'n'mix your codes! Up to THREE separate codes can be entered at one time (but only two will be needed for this game at max).
Commando and Super Joe are trademarks of Capcom USA, Inc.

Contra™ Game

We've got some real Game Genie™ goodies for Contra™—CONT Code 2 makes sure that you keep all your weapons between lives, while CONT Codes 4 thru 7 see that you get off to a good start.

CONT CODE	KEY IN . . .	EFFECT . . .
1	SLAIUZ	Start with infinite lives

refer to pages 10 and 11 for instructions. If you still have problems, call 1-513-868-8835.

45

2	GXIIUX	Keep weapons after losing a life
3	SLTIYG	Become invincible
4	PEIIXZ	Start new life with machine gun
5	ZEIIXZ	Start new life with flame-thrower
6	LEIIXZ	Start new life with spread gun
7	GEIIXZ	Start new life with laser

Remember that you can pick'n'mix your codes! Up to three separate codes can be entered at one time.
Contra is a trademark of Konami Inc.
Game Genie is a trademark of Lewis Galoob Toys, Inc.

Crystalis™ Game

CRYS Codes 1 and 2 give you gold at the start, so you can buy powerful weapons and equipment in the village before setting out on your quest. CRYS Codes 9 and 10 give you free boarding at the Inn and free goods from the shops. You must have enough money to buy what you want, but you won't be charged, so you can come back for more whenever you like!

CRYS CODE	KEY IN . . .	EFFECT . . .
1	VVOGUOSE	Start with some gold
2	NYVSPZGV	First pupil gives you more gold
3	SXNOVXSE	Magic doesn't use up M.P.
4	GZEOTGSA	Immune to most damage
5	AASVVNYA	Immune to poison
6	AEKTSNYA	Immune to paralysis
7	TEOTVYGA	Stronger poison
8	ZEOTVYGA	Weaker poison
9	SZUOIVSE + SZKPLVSE	Free boarding at Inn
10	SXVPUOSE + SXVOOOSE	Free items in shops

Remember, you can enter up to THREE separate codes at one time, or one double code (like CRYS Code 9) and one single code (like CRYS Code 5).
Crystalis is a trademark of SNK Corp of America.

Cybernoid™ Game

This game is so popular all over the world that we spent a lot of time coming up with this list of Game Genie™ codes. Just have a scan down the list and pick a couple out to customize your game. Most anything a hardened Cybernoid™ player could wish for is here.

CYBE CODE	KEY IN . . .	EFFECT . . .
1	SZVZGOVK	Start with infinite lives
2	NYEATXNY	Start with 1 life
3	UYEATXNN	Start with 5 lives
4	AAEATXNN	Start with 18 lives

Some codes may cause undesired effects (which are not permanent). If this occurs,

5	AZUALZGO + AXEXIPGO	Start with double bombs
6	GOOZZPZA	20 'genocides' on new life
7	GPUETZPA + GOOZYPPA	Start new life with 20 shields
8	GPKAZZIA + GOOXGPIA	Start with 20 seekers and bouncers
9	SZNPVOVK	Infinite bombs
10	SXEUSSVK	Infinite 'genocides'
11	SXOPUSVK	Infinite shields
12	SZNOLNVK	Infinite seekers
13	NNOEPPAE	Start with rear laser
14	GZKZZOSE	Keep rear laser after death
15	GZKXAOSE + GZKZIOSE	Keep mace after death

Remember, you can program your own codes! CYBE Codes 2 through 4 might make good codes to try your programming luck on!

Cybernoid is a trademark of Gremlin Graphics, Inc. Used by Acclaim Entertainment, Inc., under license.
Game Genie is a trademark of Lewis Galoob Toys, Inc.

Dash Galaxy in the Alien Asylum™ Game

Here's a king-size helping of DASH Codes to help you change the game in a wide range of ways. Why not use DASH Codes 5 and 11 together to practice the higher levels?

DASH CODE	KEY IN . . .	EFFECT . . .
1	SZVPTOVK	Can't lose lives in rooms
2	SZUPLOVK	Can't lose lives in elevator shaft
3	PENPIALA	Start with 1 life
4	TENPIALA	Start with 6 lives
5	PENPIALE	Start with 9 lives
6	NYSXAOAN	Oxygen used up more slowly in shaft
7	AYXXSNNY	Oxygen used up more quickly in rooms
8	AAEPZIPA	Won't take damage from shots and collisions
9	OZEPOISE + IAEPXSVI	Start on level 5
10	OZEPOISE + ZAEPXSVS	Start on level 10
11	OZEPOISE + YAEPXSVS	Start on level 15
12	OZEPOISE + GPEPXSVI	Start on level 20
13	VTNSEXSX	Infinite bombs in elevator shaft
14	VVVSXXSX	Infinite bombs in rooms
15	VVOSSXSX	Infinite detonators in shafts
16	VTESNUSX	Infinite detonators in rooms

refer to pages 10 and 11 for instructions. If you still have problems, call 1-513-868-8835.   47

| 17 | VTEZIKSX | Infinite keys in shafts |
| 18 | VVOXTOSX | Infinite keys in rooms |

Remember that you can pick'n'mix your codes! You can enter up to THREE separate codes at one time, or one double-code (like DASH Code 11) and one single code (like DASH Code 5).
Dash Galaxy in the Alien Asylum is a trademark of Data East USA, Inc.

Days of Thunder™ Game

Some excellent codes to choose from! DAYS Code 3 gives you a turbo boost—you'll reach top speed in half the time. DAYS Code 4 does the same, but better—the other racers won't see through your dust! DAYS Code 6 improves your left-hand cornering so you can now take corners at high speed without being pushed into the barrier.

DAYS
CODE	KEY IN . . .	EFFECT . . .	
1	NYKNIUNO	Start with more fuel	
2	YIKNIUNO	Start with less fuel	
3	SXEYPUSU	Faster acceleration	
4	IEUNLLLA + SXEYPUSU	Maximum acceleration	
5	AAVOEXNY	Tires don't burst	
6	SNXOSKEY	Better left-hand cornering	

Remember that you can pick'n'mix your codes.
Days of Thunder is a trademark of Paramount Pictures. Used by Mindscape Inc. under license.

Deadly Towers™ Game

DEAD Code 5 is an interesting one—when you go to the shop, you can buy whatever you like (as long as you do have enough money to pay for it) and the shopkeeper will forget to take your money! Also, DEAD Codes 3 and 4 magically transform money. Using DEAD Code 3, if you pick up 1 Ludder™, 10 will actually be added to your purse!

DEAD
CODE	KEY IN . . .	EFFECT . . .
1	LGXELPZU	Start with 75 Ludder
2	GXSONPST	You won't take any damage
3	ZEUPKYPE	Pick up 1 Ludder—it becomes 10!
4	GOUPUYIA	Pick up 5 Ludder—it becomes 20!
5	GXUGLVON	Shopkeeper forgets to charge you

Remember that you can pick'n'mix your codes! Up to three separate codes can be entered at one time.
Deadly Towers and Ludder are trademarks of Broderbund Software, Inc.

Defender II™ Game

Defender II™ is another absolutely brilliant arcade classic that gets the full Game Genie™ treatment—try DEF Code 6 for a real challenge, or DEF Code 2 for a real cake-walk. You won't get any more hassle from those Yllabian Space Guppys™ if you use these codes.

DEF
CODE	KEY IN . . .	EFFECT . . .
1	GXTGEY	Infinite lives

Some codes may cause undesired effects (which are not permanent). If this occurs,

2	GXYSGI	Infinite smart bombs
3	PELGNY	Start with 1 life
4	TELGNY	Start with 6 lives
5	PELGNN	Start with 9 lives
6	YAZVPG + YETVIL	Super speed

Remember that you can pick'n'mix your codes! You can enter up to THREE separate codes at one time, or DEF Code 6 and any other DEF Code.

Defender II and Yllabian Space Guppys are trademarks of Williams Electronics Games, Inc. Used by HAL America, Inc., under license. Game Genie is a trademark of Lewis Galoob Toys, Inc.

Defender of the Crown™ Game

Reclaim the Crown and reunite England with the help of Robin Hood and your ever-faithful Game Genie™! Use CROW Codes 3 thru 8 to change the price of men, catapults and castles— the higher the cost, the harder the game will be.

CROW CODE	KEY IN . . .	EFFECT . . .
1	ZAVVALGO	Only 10 soldiers in your Garrison
2	AZVVALGO	40 soldiers in your Garrison
3	AAEOUPPA	Soldiers for free
4	LAEOUPPA	Triple the cost of soldiers
5	GAEOKOAA	Halve the cost of knights
6	APEOKOAA	Double the cost of knights
7	YAEOSOYA	Halve the cost of catapults
8	ZAEOVPGO	Halve the cost of castles

Game Genie programmers will have a lot of fun here. Try adjusting all the codes to suit your every need!

Defender of the Crown is a trademark of Cinemaware Corp.
Game Genie is a trademark of Lewis Galoob Toys, Inc.

Demon Sword™ Game

There are loads of Game Genie™ codes for this one! DEM Codes 7 thru 11 warp you thru the levels, while DEM Codes 12 thru 16 can give you a real head start. DEM Code 1 gives you infinite powers and lives, which is just what you need to explore the game fully.

DEM CODE	KEY IN . . .	EFFECT . . .
1	AESVLTPA	Infinite powers and lives
2	SXSIYASA	Infinite lives
3	AEVSUIZA	Start game with 1 life
4	IEVSUIZA	Start game with 6 lives
5	AEVSUIZE	Start game with 9 lives
6	SZKGTTSA	Infinite life energy

7	PANZLPAA + ATNXAOSA	Start on level 2
8	ZANZLPAA + ATNXAOSA	Start on level 3
9	LANZLPAA + ATNXAOSA	Start on level 4
10	GANZLPAA + ATNXAOSA	Start on level 5
11	IANZLPAA + ATNXAOSA	Start on level 6
12	XZNZGPSA + VEEZYOSE	Start with 44 red spheres
13	XZNZGPSA + VEEXZOSE	Start with 44 black spheres
14	XZNZGPSA + VANXLOSE	Start with 44 fire spheres
15	XZNZGPSA + VANXTOSE	Start with 44 lightning bolts
16	XZNZGPSA + VEEZPOSE	Start with 44 power beams
17	VTVTAESX	Phoenix ALWAYS rescues you
18	SLNNANSO	Infinite fire/lightning/ power beams on pick up
19	VTNXAOSE	Extra dart strength

Remember that you can pick'n'mix your codes! You can enter up to THREE separate codes at one time, or one double-code (like DEM Code 9) and one single code (like DEM Code 1).

Demon Sword is a trademark of Taito America Corporation.
Game Genie is a trademark of Lewis Galoob Toys, Inc.

Destination Earthstar™ Game

If you are already a pro at this game, you could try STAR Codes 1 and 3 together. But if you still need help, never fear–STAR Code 2 gives you more energy and STAR Code 4 gives you infinite lives!

STAR CODE	KEY IN . . .	EFFECT . . .
1	ISNEUUOP	Less energy
2	NNNEUUOO	More energy
3	PAVTXGLA	Start game with 1 life
4	SXVSVIVG	Infinite lives
5	XTNVSNXK	Don't lose special weapon in sub game

Destination Earthstar is a trademark of Acclaim Entertainment Inc.

Dick Tracy™ Game

TRACY Code 1—infinite handgun bullets—gives you a much better chance of survival. TRACY Code 2 gives you double the usual amount of super punches on pick-up and is great when combined with TRACY Code 4—infinite energy. And for super agility, check out TRACY Code 8—mega-jump. It will let you jump right over your enemies and their bullets and across some very large gaps, too!

TRACY CODE	KEY IN . . .	EFFECT . . .
1	SZXZEOVK	Infinite hand gun bullets
2	GOEPIOZA	More super punches on pick-up
3	SZKZIXVK	Infinite super punches
4	GXVOINSV	Infinite energy

Some codes may cause undesired effects (which are not permanent). If this occurs,

5	AOVOGNAU	Take more damage
6	SXVXZEVK	Infinite machine gun bullets
7	SZEXIXVK	Infinite tear gas
8	KYVZAANY	Mega-jumping Dick Tracy™

Dick Tracy is a trademark of The Walt Disney Company. Used by Bandai America, Inc. under license.

Dig Dug™ II: Trouble in Paradise™ Game

Now you can play Dig Dug™ II the way YOU want to! We think that DIG Code 7 is the best, but try the codes for yourself to decide.

DIG CODE	KEY IN . . .	EFFECT . . .
1	GZETIZEI	Instant inflate and explode!
2	PEETOPLA	Start with 1 life—both players
3	AEETOPLE	Start with 8 lives—both players
4	SZXLSVVK	Never lose lives from touching water
5	SXVKLVVK	Never lose lives from Fygar's™ flame
6	SXNIPEVK	Never lose lives from hitting enemies
7	OZNYPUPX + ZANYZLLA	Turbo speed . . .

Remember that you can pick'n'mix your codes! You can use DIG Code 7 and any single DIG Code, or up to THREE of the other DIG Codes at the same time!

Dig Dug, Trouble in Paradise and Fygar are trademarks of Namco Ltd.

Dirty Harry™ Game

Well, it's time to make Harry's™ day and yours too, with some helpful Codes to defeat the evil Anaconda™. HARRY Code 4 should be a great help for the ones who need it. HARRY Codes 6 and 7 will adjust the number of bullets your Magnum can use—you can restrict it to make things more difficult, or increase it for more blasting power!

HARRY CODE	KEY IN . . .	EFFECT . . .
1	SXUKOKVK	Infinite lives
2	PANSGIIA	1 life
3	ZANSGIIE	10 lives
4	GXXGXGST	Infinite energy
5	AEVLIPZA	Maximum energy from Chili Dogs
6	ZESSTSPO + ZEVIZSPO	Only 10 Magnum Bullets allowed
7	ZUSSTSPP + ZUVIZSPP	50 Magnum Bullets allowed

Remember that you can pick'n'mix your codes. You can enter up to THREE separate codes at one time.

Dirty Harry and Anaconda are trademarks of Warner Bros. Inc.

Disney's Duck Tales™ Game

Here are some DUCK Codes to make Uncle Scrooge™ better than the average duck! You can have double strength feathers with DUCK Code 6, or make time stand still with DUCK Code 8. For any gamers that need all the help they can get, using DUCK Codes 1 and 8 together is a must!

DUCK CODE	KEY IN . . .	EFFECT . . .	
1	SXUIEKVK	Infinite lives	
2	ATVVXLEZ	Infinite hit points	
3	AAESULZA	Start with 1 life	
4	IAESULZA	Start with 6 lives	
5	AAESULZE	Start with 9 lives	
6	LAVTNLPA	Lose half normal hit points (in easy game)	
7	ZAXSKLIE + SXNIUKOU + SZNISESU	Double usual time	
8	OVUVAZSV	Freeze timer	

Remember that you can pick'n'mix your codes! You can enter up to THREE separate codes at one time, or one triple-code (like DUCK Code 7).

Disney's Duck Tales and Uncle Scrooge are trademarks of Walt Disney Company. Used by Capcom USA, Inc., under license

Donkey Kong™ Game

If you are playing the Donkey Kong Classics™ pack, then look at the entry for Donkey Kong Classics (next page). These Game Genie™ codes are for the ORIGINAL version of Donkey Kong™.

DK3 CODE	KEY IN . . .	EFFECT . . .	
1	SXNGOZVG	Infinite lives	
2	PENKNPLA	Start with 1 life	
3	PENKNPLE	Start with 9 lives	

Donkey Kong and Donkey Kong Classics are trademarks of Nintendo of America, Inc.
Game Genie is a trademark of Lewis Galoob Toys, Inc.

Donkey Kong 3™ Game

Try to beat the game using 9 lives (DK3 Code 3) before you go for infinite lives (DK3 Code 1). When you've done that, try playing with only 1 life (DK3 Code 2). DK3 Codes 5 thru 7 all improve your shooting power and are great when used together. Want to make bees explode when you shoot them? Try DK3 Code 8—and watch out for flying debris!

DK3 CODE	KEY IN . . .	EFFECT . . .	
1	SZNKOPVI	Start with infinite lives	
2	PEEGITLA	Start with 1 life	
3	PEEGITLE	Start with 9 lives	
4	ZEKKGYEE	Reduce the time for pros	
5	ZAOSZAPA	Normal spray more powerful	
6	ZLOSLAAA	Normal spray longer	
7	AASSYPPA	Spray cuts through baddies	

     Some codes may cause undesired effects (which are not permanent). If this occurs,

| 8 | AAKVZALL | Normal bees explode | |
| 9 | TEXKVGLA | Speeding Stanley™ | |

Remember that you can pick'n'mix your codes—why not try DK3 Code 2 and DK3 Code 4 together and see if you can beat your old high score?
Donkey Kong 3 and Stanley are trademarks of Nintendo of America, Inc.

Donkey Kong Classics™ Game

These codes are unique to the games on the Donkey Kong Classics™ pack—if you are playing the pack that has Donkey Kong™ by itself, then look under Donkey Kong (previous page). But as long as you're here, check out CLAS Codes 5 and 11—they let you control your jump, even change direction in mid-air! CLAS Code 13 makes climbing faster to help you escape the baddies, and CLAS Code 14 lets you jump down from the vines with no problem.
IMPORTANT: CODES FOR DONKEY KONG JR.™ ARE ONLY FOR THE DONKEY KONG CLASSICS™ PACK VERSION.

CLAS CODE	KEY IN . . .	EFFECT . . .	
DONKEY KONG™			
1	SXYAOP	Infinite lives	
2	PETANA	Start with 1 life	
3	TETANA	Start with 6 lives	
4	PETANE	Start with 9 lives	
5	AEVAVSIA	Controllable jump	
6	EAKOLSLG	Keep hammer for longer	
DONKEY KONG JR.™			
7	SZZGTP	Infinite lives	
8	PATLST	Start with 1 life	
9	TATLST	Start with 6 lives	
10	PATLSV	Start with 9 lives	
11	AEKGAUIA	Controllable jump	
12	EXSKSGEY + EXUKNGEY	Speed up	
13	EAVGVIAG	Faster single vine climbing	
14	PAXIPAIA	Can fall onto platforms	

Remember that you can pick'n'mix your codes!
Donkey Kong Classics, Donkey Kong and Donkey Kong Jr. are trademarks of Nintendo of America Inc.

Double Dragon™ Game

We have a selection of codes to affect the timer in this game—you can do anything from making it count down faster to freezing it altogether. Also, DUB Codes 5 and 6 are good fun if used in a 2-player, head-to-head mode B game—you can give either player an advantage using the relevant code, or make them both super-strong.

DUB CODE	KEY IN . . .	EFFECT . . .	
1	AAUNYLPA	Freeze the timer countdown	
2	AEUTLZZA	Start game with 1 life	
3	IEUTLZZA	Start game with 6 lives	
4	AEUTLZZE	Start game with 9 lives	
5	XTKNXEZK	More energy for player 2 or the CPU	
6	XTKYOEZK	More energy for player 1	
7	AZUYZLAL	Timer will count down fast	
8	APUYZLAL	Timer will count down super-fast	

Remember that you can pick'n'mix your codes! Up to three separate codes can be entered at one time.

Double Dragon is a trademark of Tradewest, Inc.

Double Dragon II: The Revenge™ Game

A wickedly hard game deserves some wickedly clever Game Genie™ codes—and that's just what you've got! You can warp to any mission, including the mysterious Mission 9 . . .The Final Confrontation! Just use DD2 Codes 8 thru 12 to do this. You can also make sure that you never die using DD2 Codes 5 thru 7, or start with 8 lives by using DD2 Codes 1 and 2! Not bad, eh?

DD2 CODE	KEY IN . . .	EFFECT . . .	
1	AASVETGE	Player 1 starts with 8 lives	
2	AAVVSTGE	Player 2 starts with 8 lives	
3	PASVETGA	Player 1 starts with 1 life	
4	PAVVSTGA	Player 2 starts with 1 life	
5	SZXAYKVS	Never lose lives from falling	
6	SXOANXVS	Never lose lives from low energy	
7	SZVESUVS	Never lose lives from water	
8	LAUTXTAA	Start on mission 4	
9	IAUTXTAA	Start on mission 5	
10	TAUTXTAA	Start on mission 6	
11	PAUTXTAE	Start on mission 7	
12	TAUTXTAE	Start on mission 9	
13	NNEVOIAE	Slow down gameplay	

Remember that you can pick'n'mix your codes! You can enter up to THREE separate codes at one time.

Double Dragon II: The Revenge is a trademark of Technos Japan Corporation. Used by Acclaim Entertainment Inc., under license. Game Genie is a trademark of Lewis Galoob Toys, Inc.

Double Dragon III—The Sacred Stones™ Game

Some great codes here for this mega-difficult game. DD3 Code 1 gives you protection when you get into hand-to-hand combat. DD3 Code 7 makes sure each player's special weapons never run out! And to improve your fighting abilities, be sure to check out DD3 Code 11. It makes your

    Some codes may cause undesired effects (which are not permanent). If this occurs,

weapons and your punch much stronger and gives you high kick. But be careful, 'cause it makes those end-of-level guardians stronger too!

DD3

CODE	KEY IN . . .	EFFECT . . .	
1	SZUUPAAX	Protection for Billy™, Jimmy™ & Chin™	
2	GVEPXGGI	More energy for Billy & Jimmy	
3	GVEOXKZG	More energy for Ranzou™	
4	ZXEPXGGS	Less energy for Billy & Jimmy	
5	IXEOXKZG	Less energy for Ranzou	
6	ZUEONGGT	Less energy for Chin	
7	AAELIGPA + GZXUPUVS	Infinite 'special' weapons for all	
8	GOOPKGIA	Start with 20 special weapons for Billy, Jimmy & Chin	
9	AXOPKGIE	Start with 40 special weapons for Billy, Jimmy & Chin	
10	AXOONGGO	Start with 40 special weapons for Ranzou	
11	OZVLGASX	More powerful punch and weapon, and high kick!	

Remember that you can pick 'n' mix your codes. You can enter up to THREE separate codes at one time, or one double code (like DD3 Code 7) and one single code (like DD3 Code 11).

Double Dragon III—The Sacred Stones, Billy, Jimmy, Chin and Ranzou are trademarks of Technos Japan Corporation. Used by Acclaim Entertainment, Inc. under license.

Dr. Chaos™ Game

CHAOS Code 1 starts you off with 99 life points and CHAOS Code 3 starts you with the Shield Suit. CHAOS Code 4—mega-jump—lets you jump right over the monsters and also gives you access to some extra rooms! CHAOS Code 6 increases the time you are invincible after touching a monster, and CHAOS Code 7 reduces it, so you can get hit again right away!

CHAOS

CODE	KEY IN . . .	EFFECT . . .	
1	LTKKVPZL	Start with more energy	
2	PPKKVPZU	Start with less energy	
3	PASKSPAA + ZISKNPLG	Start with Shield Suit	
4	AEEGUZLE	Mega-jump	
5	GXKIKIST	Immune to damage	
6	AKSSKIGP	More invincibility time	
7	GESSKIGP	Less invincibility time	
8	OVKIKISV + PEKISIGY	Take minimal damage	
9	TVOSSITG + AEOSKIYA	Take more damage and Shield Suit has no effect	
10	GZEYEEVK	Infinite pistol bullets	

Remember that you can pick'n'mix your codes. You can enter up to THREE separate codes at one time, or one double code (like CHAOS Code 3) and one single code (like CHAOS Code 6).

Dr. Chaos is a trademark of Fujisankei Communications International, Inc.

Dr. Jekyll and Mr. Hyde™ Game

HYDE Code 4 lets you start each game instantly instead of sitting through the presentation sequence, while HYDE code 3 makes sure that you keep all your coins between games, so the total gradually mounts up as you play through a session.

HYDE CODE	KEY IN . . .	EFFECT . . .	
1	GZXVTKVK + GZXTTSVK	Complete invincibility!	
2	KENLKVSE	Start with 16 coins	
3	GXNLKVSE	Keep coins from previous games	
4	NXNSZEOO	Instant game restart	

Remember, you can program your own codes! HYDE Code 2 might make a good code to try your programming luck on!

Dr. Jekyll and Mr. Hyde is a trademark of Bandai America, Inc.

Dragon Power™ Game

DRAG Code 1 gives you infinite energy, which will come in handy for exploring the game. Normally when you start a game, you have no Wind Waves™—use DRAG Code 3 and you'll have 24 right away! DRAG Code 2 gives you 128 energy units instead of the usual 100 at the start of a game.

DRAG CODE	KEY IN . . .	EFFECT . . .	
1	SZVOSZVG	Start with infinite energy	
2	EAXAILGT	Start with extra energy	
3	KAOETLSA	Start with 24 Wind Waves	

Remember that you can pick'n'mix your codes—Try using DRAG Codes 1 and 3 or DRAG Codes 2 and 3 together.

Dragon Power and Wind Waves are trademarks of Bandai America, Inc.

Dragon Warrior™ Game

This is a very large, challenging and rewarding game—it can take a long time and many tries to reach the really good parts. Why not use some of the WAR Codes to let you explore a little? You could try WAR Code 3—you'll start with extra money to buy excellent equipment from the start!

WAR CODE	KEY IN . . .	EFFECT . . .	
1	SXOIVLSA	Infinite Magic Power™	
2	AEVGUIZA	Take no damage in swamp	
3	VVOYYTSA	Start with 256 gold coins	
4	VKOIVLSA	All spells use only one magic point	
5	YAKKEVYA	Barriers cause half usual damage	

Dragon Warrior and Magic Power are trademarks of Nintendo of America, Inc.

Some codes may cause undesired effects (which are not permanent). If this occurs,

Dungeon Magic™ Game

MAGIC Code 1 reduces your battle damage and MAGIC Code 3 gives you plenty of gold at the start. With MAGIC Code 5, casting spells uses up no energy—once you learn a spell you can use it as many times as you like. MAGIC Codes 6, 7 and 8 let you stay at the Inn and have items at the shop and armory for free. You must have enough money to buy what you want, but you won't be charged, so you can go back for more whenever you like!

MAGIC CODE	KEY IN . . .	EFFECT . . .	
1	OVVLGLSV + ZEVLIUYL	Take less damage	
2	SXVLTLSA	Take no damage	
3	GTKIITAA	Start with 100 gold pieces	
4	ZAKIITAA + PGKSGTAG	Start with 512 gold pieces	
5	SZXVXASA	Casting spells uses up no energy	
6	PXSTLZPG + AXSTYZAG	Stay at the Inn for free	
7	PXUVXTPG + AXUVVTAG	Items at Grocer's shop are free	
8	PXENPLPG + AXENILAG	Items at Armory are free	

Remember that you can pick'n'mix your codes. You can enter up to THREE separate codes at one time or one double code (like Magic Code 4) and one single code (like Magic Code 5).
Dungeon Magic is a trademark of Taito America Corp.

Dynowarz—The Destruction of Spondylus™ Game

The war has begun, and guess whose side Game Genie™ is on? DYNO Code 1 makes you invincible—well almost, so watch out! You can start on different levels with DYNO Codes 5 thru 8. Also, check out DYNO Codes 9 and 10, for a most excellent mega-jump and super speed!

DYNO CODE	KEY IN . . .	EFFECT . . .	
1	PANSAEPX + GZNITAVG	Mostly invincible	
2	ATSIOGSZ	No harm from spikes	
3	AAVNVPLA	No harm from any dinosaur	
4	AVNTNKXA	Infinite shield	
5	TAXGLPPA	Start at level 2	
6	ZAXGLPPE	Start at level 3	
7	TAXGLPPE	Start at level 4	
8	ZPXGLPPA	Start at level 5	
9	YEXIYLLA	Mega-jump power	
10	LANSIZPA	Speed up left and right	

Remember that you can pick'n'mix. Try to figure out how to start at other levels by changing DYNO Codes 5 thru 8!
Dynowarz—The Destruction of Spondylus is a trademark of Bandai America, Inc.
Game Genie is a trademark of Lewis Galoob Toys, Inc.

Elevator Action™ Game

Elevator Action™ is always fun when you play it with a friend, but what if they aren't quite the game master that you are? Why, that's easy . . . we've got a whole bunch of Game Genie™ codes to load the game in either player's favor! Try ELEV Code 3 for yourself and ELEV Code 6 for your friend. ELEV Code 7 slows you down, making entering rooms easier, while ELEV Code 8 speeds you up so you can outrun the enemy and dodge their bullets!

ELEV CODE	KEY IN ...	EFFECT ...
1	GXEUOUVK	Player 1 has infinite lives
2	AAULNLZA	Player 1 starts with 1 life
3	IAULNLZA	Player 1 starts with 6 lives
4	AAULNLZE	Player 1 starts with 9 lives
5	IEVUULZA	Player 2 starts with 6 lives
6	AEVUULZE	Player 2 starts with 9 lives
7	PESIAYLA + NNUSZNSN	Slower man
8	IESIAYLA + XNUSZNSN	Faster man
9	GASTLPTA	Can only shoot one bullet
10	ZAVTLOAE + VYVTYOEY	Faster bullets
11	GAVTLOAA + KYVTYOEN	Slower bullets
12	GEONGPZA + XNXNGOVN	Faster enemy
13	PEONGPZA + NNXNGOVN	Slower enemy

Remember that you can pick'n'mix your codes.

Elevator Action is a trademark of Taito America Corporation.
Game Genie is a trademark of Lewis Galoob Toys, Inc.

Excitebike™ Game

Plenty of great Game Genie™ codes for this motorcycle motocross game. BIKE Code 1 gives you a special engine cooling system that lets you race faster, while BIKE Code 2 reduces the annoying delay when you wipe out, and there are two types of turbo chargers available with BIKE Codes 3 and 4. You can also change the number of enemy bikes and the time limits with BIKE Codes 5 thru 7. Lastly, when you use BIKE Code 4, you can jump so high that strange things happen—watch out!

BIKE CODE	KEY IN ...	EFFECT ...
1	SXXTYUVV	Never overheat
2	YEXIKOYA	Recover fast after crashes
3	ENUKGEAP + GESGPALA	Turbo speed on 'A' button
4	EVUKGEAP + TESGPALA	Mega turbo speed on 'A' button
5	PEXIEZLA	Reduced enemy bikes in game B
6	AAUSEYAO	Timer runs at half speed
7	GAUSEYAP	Timer runs at quarter speed

Remember that you can pick'n'mix your codes! You can enter up to THREE separate codes at one time, or one double-code (like BIKE Code 3) and one single code (like BIKE Code 1)

Excitebike is a trademark of Nintendo of America Inc.
Game Genie is a trademark of Lewis Galoob Toys, Inc.

Some codes may cause undesired effects (which are not permanent). If this occurs,

Exodus Ultima™ Game

We've got some great codes for Exodus Ultima™, but a couple of them are gonna need some explaining . . . ULT Code 2 makes sure there is no limit on the amount of stat points you can give to any one attribute of your character; that is, you aren't limited to the usual 25. ULT Code 9 makes sure that you never lose your weapons, but they will go if you sell them!

ULT CODE	KEY IN . . .	EFFECT . . .	
1	GZUKOGST	Take no damage from most monsters	
2	AEOAKVAA	No limit on stat points	
3	YKEAUVTZ + LKUAVYZU + LGSOPAZU	75 stat points to start, not 50	
4	LSEAUVTX + YSUAVYZU + YISOPAZU9	5 stat points to start, not 50	
5	IEOPTPPA	Start with 5 of each item	
6	ZEOPTPPE	Start with 10 of each item	
7	EKEOAPGV	Start with 200 GPs	
8	ZEEOAPGT + PUEPTPAL	Start with 512 GPs	
9	AAXIAPPA	Never lose weapons	
10	KPVSUZOP	Never lose magic	
11	AAUEPYPA + OLUAGYOI	Rapid magic recovery	

Remember, you can program your own codes! ULT Codes 5 and 6 might make good codes to try your programming luck on!

Exodus Ultima is a trademark of Richard Garriot. Used by Fujisankei Communications International, Inc., under license

Fantasy Zone™ Game

Program some variety! You can start on different levels that you may not have seen yet by using FAN Codes 8 through 13. Fan Code 5 eliminates the time limit on bought weapons, and FAN Code 6 will let you keep weapons—even if you lose a life, until your next visit to the shop!

FAN CODE	KEY IN . . .	EFFECT . . .	
1	OZEVYTVK	Infinite lives	
2	PAXVOPLA	Start with 1 life	
3	TAXVOPLA	Start with 6 lives	
4	PAXVOPLE	Start with 9 lives	
5	OXETOAVK	Keep bought weapon for a life	
6	OXETOAVK + OGOVATSE	Keep bought weapon until next shop visit	
7	AAOVKTPA	Autofire on all weapons	
8	PASVYYAA	Start on level 2	
9	ZASVYYAA	Start on level 3	
10	LASVYYAA	Start on level 4	
11	GASVYYAA	Start on level 5	
12	IASVYYAA	Start on level 6	
13	TASVYYAA	Start on level 7	

refer to pages 10 and 11 for instructions. If you still have problems, call 1-513-868-8835.

Remember that you can pick'n'mix your codes! You can enter up to THREE separate codes at one time, or one double-code (like FAN Code 6) and one single code (like FAN Code 7).
Fantasy Zone is a trademark of Sega Enterprises Ltd.

Faxanadu™ Game

FAX Codes 1, 4 and 7 will each give you a very big advantage. However, some of these codes will set you back, so choose carefully. Also note that with FAX Codes 4, 5 and 6, you will need to see the King before you can obtain your Gold!

FAX CODE	KEY IN . . .	EFFECT . . .
1	GXOGZESV + GXOKLESV	Infinite power
2	AXXSNTAP	Double starting power
3	AUXSNTAP	Triple starting power
4	SXXNUOSE + SXUYUOSE + SXUNUOSE	Infinite Gold
5	IASEPSZA	Half normal amount of Gold
6	GPSEPSZA	Double normal amount of Gold
7	AEENEZZA	Infinite magic
8	AAUTAEOY + AAKTPAKY + AAUTZAPA	Slow mode
9	AVXVGPSZ	Jump in direction you are facing

Remeber that you can pick'n'mix your codes. You can enter up to THREE separate codes at one time, or one triple code (like FAX Code 4), or one double code (like FAX Code 1) plus one single code (like FAX Code 2).
Faxanadu is a trademark of Falcom. Used by Hudson Soft, Inc. under license.

Final Fantasy™ Game

We have a lot of codes for this excellent fantasy adventure! FINAL Codes 1 and 2 will allow you to use the two spells without using up any valuable Magic Points. With FINAL Code 5, all character classes will be able to wield magic powers! FINAL Codes 7 thru 36 will let you adjust the attributes of all the character classes. You can also program in your own values. You can have a strong Black Mage™, or a weak Fighter! The choices are limitless!

FINAL CODE	KEY IN . . .	EFFECT . . .
1	SZULIEVS	"LIFE" Spell never uses up Magic Points
2	SZVULEVS	"LIF2" Spell never uses up Magic Points
3	TESGTYZA	Magic Users start with 6 Magic Points
4	PESGTYZE	Magic Users start with 9 Magic Points
5	ELEXVLEY + AESGANGA + AESGGNAA	Any Character can use any Magic

Some codes may cause undesired effects (which are not permanent). If this occurs,

6	AZOUGAEP + LAOUIAPA	Start with 800 Gold
7	TGKLPALZ	Double Fighter Hit Points
8	GPKLPEZA	Double Fighter's Damage
9	GPKUAEZA	Double Fighter's Hit
10	ZTKUPAIU	Double Fighter's Evade
11	ZAKLTAIE	Double Fighter's Luck
12	GLSLPETO	Double Thief's Hit Points
13	TASLYAZA	Triple Thief's Damage
14	ZASUAAIE	Double Thief's Hit
15	GYSUPEZL	Double Thief's Evade
16	TPSLTEYE	Double Thief's Luck
17	ZGVLPAPZ	Double Black Belt's Hit Points
18	TAVLYAZA	Triple Black Belt's Damage
19	ZAVUAAIE	Double Black Belt's Hit
20	ZTVUPAIU	Double Black Belt's Evade
21	ZAVLTAIE	Double Black Belt's Luck
22	GLNLPETO	Double Red Mage™'s Hit Points
23	ZANLYAIE	Double Red Mage's Damage
24	TANUAAYE	Double Red Mage's Hit
25	GYNUPEZL	Double Red Mage's Evade
26	ZANLTAIE	Double Red Mage's Luck
27	AUELPEGO	Double White Mage™'s Hit Points
28	TEELYAZA	Triple White Mage's Damage
29	ZEEUAAIE	Double White Mage's Hit
30	ZVEUPAIU	Double White Mage's Evade
31	ZEELTAIE	Double White Mage's Luck
32	ZUOLPEPP	Double Black Mage's Hit Points
33	LEOLYAPA	Triple Black Mage's Damage
34	ZEOUAAIE	Double Black Mage's Hit
35	GNOUPEZL	Double Black Mage's Evade
36	GOOLTEZA	Double Black Mage's Luck
37	GXSZPKSV + GXSXZKSV	Infinite Gold

Take your time picking and mixing. There are lots of codes to choose from!
Final Fantasy, Black Mage, Red Mage and White Mage are trademarks of Square Soft, Inc.

Fist of the North Star™ Game

There are many ways to change the difficulty of the game—try using FIST Codes 1 thru 4 to select the number of lives that Ken™ has. You can make Ken tougher with FIST Codes 7 and 11, and you can also make him stronger with FIST Codes 8 thru 10, or even change the time limit with FIST Code 5. For some fun, try FIST Code 12 and see what happens.

FIST

CODE	KEY IN ...	EFFECT ...	
1	SXKKYPVG	Infinite lives	
2	PEKKGALA	Start with 1 life	
3	TEKKGALA	Start with 6 lives	
4	PEKKGALE	Start with 9 lives	
5	SZSVGTVG	Freeze timer	
6	OTSGOGSV	For pro's—one hit kills you!	
7	OTSGOGSV + PASGXKOI	Take minimum damage from all enemies	
8	TEELTPPA	Sweep kick damages enemies more	
9	AEOLGPLE	Straight kick damages enemies more	
10	OVOUZPSV + ZEOULOOS	Any attack mega-damages enemies	
11	AAUKVGGA	Can't be knocked back by big thugs	
12	EISGUPEY	Pogo stick	

Remember that you can pick'n'mix your codes! You can enter up to THREE separate codes at one time, or one double-code (like FIST Code 10) and one single code (like FIST Code 4).

Fist of the North Star and Ken are trademarks of Toei Animation. Used by Taxan USA Corp. under license

Flying Dragon™—The Secret Scroll™ Game

Getting thru to the World Tournament is always difficult, but judicious use of some of these Game Genie™ codes will make things easier.

FLY

CODE	KEY IN ...	EFFECT ...	
1	VEKLTAKZ	Start with infinite lives	
2	GXEEEPVG	Start with infinite time	
3	PANATALA	Start with 1 life	
4	TANATALA	Start with 6 lives	
5	PANATALE	Start with 9 lives	
6	TAOXULLA	Start with double KO power	

Remember that you can pick'n'mix your codes! Up to three separate codes can be entered at one time.

Flying Dragon and The Secret Scroll are trademarks of Culture Brain USA Inc.
Game Genie is a trademark of Lewis Galoob Toys, Inc.

    Some codes may cause undesired effects (which are not permanent). If this occurs,

Freedom Force™ Game

This is a brilliant Light Gun game, the best yet! Of course we have some Game Genie™ codes to make it even better. FREE Codes 3 and 4 let you adjust how many errors you can make; you can have fewer or an infinite amount! For all-pro shooters, make the game harder by using FREE Code 9.

FREE CODE	KEY IN . . .	EFFECT . . .	
1	ZOOTYTGZ	Start with half ammo	
2	AEUTLYZZ	Infinite ammo	
3	LEOVAYTA	Fewer errors allowed	
4	OXOTYNOK	Infinite errors allowed	
5	ZAUTLTPA	Start at level 2	
6	LAUTLTPA	Start at level 3	
7	GAUTLTPA	Start at level 4	
8	IAUTLTPA	Start at level 5	
9	GAKVYVAO	Start with half health	
10	GZVAYLSA	Infinite health	

Remember that you can pick'n'mix your codes! You can enter up to THREE separate codes at one time.

Freedom Force is a trademark of The Nylint Corporation.
Game Genie is a trademark of Lewis Galoob Toys, Inc.

Friday the 13th™ Game

Now it doesn't matter if you lose a few children, because 13TH Code 1 will give you as many as you need! As you look down the list, bear in mind that whenever the "active counselor" is mentioned, we are referring to the counselor that you currently control.

13TH CODE	KEY IN . . .	EFFECT . . .	
1	SZSLUEVK + IYKLSEAY	Infinite children	
2	IEVANTPA + YUNESVYA	Start with 55 children	
3	OTEIVISV	Infinite energy for active counselor	
4	ZZOUAGTE	Vitamins heal active counselor better	
5	AZEVXLGE	Vitamins heal others better	
6	INNLIZGY	Autofire	
7	SZVLGXOU + YPVLIXAV	Turbo running	
8	GAEUZIAE	Everyone can jump high!	

Remember that you can pick'n'mix your codes!

Friday the 13th is a trademark of Paramount Pictures Corporation. Used by LJN Toys, Ltd., under license

Galaga™ Demons of Death™ Game

There are some really good Game Genie™ codes for this faithful arcade conversion . . . GALA Code 4 lets you change things so that the next wave of Galaga™ aliens will advance when you press the START button. It may cause strange effects, but it's definitely a great code! GALA Code 9 is also a real goody—now you can get those challenge stages down before your next tournament match.

GALA CODE	KEY IN . . .	EFFECT . . .	
1	XVOKVUXK	Infinite lives	
2	PAKKKILA	Start with 1 life	
3	TAKKKILA	Start with 6 lives	
4	KPNIPZEA + GANIZZIA + AAVSIZPA	Press START for next wave	
5	GGVSGXOX + EZVSIZPE + UGVSTZSE	Press START for extra life	
6	OXSTZPSX + YESTLOPY	Can't be caught by tractor beam!	
7	GXEVPAEI	Start with twin shots	
8	ATNVSAVZ	Become invincible	
9	GXOKOTEI	Play challenge stages only	

Remember that you can pick'n'mix your codes—try using GALA Code 7 with GALA Code 9 to practice the challenge stages.
Galaga and Demons of Death are trademarks of Namco Ltd.
Game Genie is a trademark of Lewis Galoob Toys, Inc.

Gauntlet II™ Game

GAUNT Codes 1 and 2 provide protection against monsters, and GAUNT Code 3 makes the poison a lot less harmful. For plenty of extra super shots, check out GAUNT Code 6. And to prolong the protective powers of the special amulets, try GAUNT Codes 7, 9 and 11.

GAUNT CODE	KEY IN . . .	EFFECT . . .	
1	OTXSSYSV	Don't take damage from monsters	
2	OTXSSYSV + ZAXSVYAA	Take less damage from monsters	
3	ZLVVVIGT	Weaker poison	
4	EGVVVIGV	Stronger poison	
5	IAUTEUZA	5 super shots picked up	
6	GPUTEUZA	20 super shots picked up	
7	AYETVUGU	Invincibility lasts longer	
8	LPETVUGU	Invincibility doesn't last as long	
9	ANNTUXGU	Repulsiveness lasts longer	
10	LONTUXGU	Repulsiveness doesn't last as long	
11	AYOTKUGU	Invisibility lasts longer	
12	LPOTKUGU	Invisibility doesn't last as long	

Remember that you can pick'n'mix your codes.
Gauntlet II is a trademark of Atari Games Corp.

Some codes may cause undesired effects (which are not permanent). If this occurs,

Ghostbusters™ Game

Who needs more spooky power, then? We've got a good selection of game boosters here—GB Codes 2 and 7 are our favorites!

GB CODE	KEY IN . . .	EFFECT . . .	
1	AVVETNTI	Start with $1,000,000	
2	SXKZAZVG	Infinite fuel	
3	OXOXKPVK	Immune to ghosts on Zuul™ stairway	
4	PAEEXKPX	Permanent ghost alarm	
5	PASPLOPX	Permanent ghost vacuum	
6	OXSESGSX	Self-emptying traps	
7	AEEZOAPA	Super sprinting up Zuul stairway	

Remember that you can pick'n'mix your codes—you can enter up to THREE separate GB Codes at the same time.

Ghostbusters and Zuul are trademarks of Columbia Pictures Industries, Inc. Used by Activision, Inc., under license

Ghostbusters™ II Game

The Game Genie™ is gonna bust the Ghostbusters™! BUST Code 7 gives you the chance to start the game with a rapid-firing proton rifle, while BUST Codes 9 and 10 give the Ectomobile™ armor plating! You can also change your number of lives and continues using BUST Codes 1 thru 6—or for some high-flying try BUST Code 8.

BUST CODE	KEY IN . . .	EFFECT . . .	
1	SUKYAUVS	Infinite lives	
2	AAXVGGLA	Start with 1 life	
3	IAXVGGLA	Start with 6 lives	
4	AAXVGGLE	Start with 9 lives	
5	SZXPSXVK	Infinite continues	
6	TAEGTAZA	Triple continues	
7	ZEEOOXYO	Rapid-firing proton rifle	
8	KYSOKXVN	All Ghostbusters can mega-jump	
9	NNXXAPAS	Shield lasts longer—car scenes	
10	SZOXLNVK	Infinite shield—car scenes	

Remember, you can program your own codes! BUST Codes 2 through 4 might make good codes to try your programming luck on!

Ghostbusters and Ectomobile are trademarks of Columbia Pictures Industries, Inc. Used by Activision, Inc., under license.
Game Genie is a trademark of Lewis Galoob Toys, Inc.

Ghosts 'n Goblins™ Game

You can change this game in some interesting ways. Try GOB Code 6 to make things real hectic, or GOB Code 7 for a slow game. You should be able to program other codes to change the speed to your own liking.

GOB CODE	KEY IN . . .	EFFECT . . .	
1	PAEKPTLA	1 life for players 1 and 2	
2	TAEKPTLA	6 lives for players 1 and 2	
3	PAEKPTLE	9 lives for players 1 and 2	
4	SZEGNOVK	Infinite lives for players 1 and 2	
5	VAEKZVSE	4 lives for player 1 only	
6	ZAKILZLA	Speed up game	
7	GAKILZLA	Slow down game	
8	SXOITUVK	Stop timer	

Remember, you can program your own codes! GOB Codes 5, 6 and 7 might make good codes to try your programming luck on!

Ghost 'n Goblins is a trademark of Capcom USA, Inc.

Gilligan's Island™ Game

GILL Codes 1 and 4 start you off with extra food and ropes. This will save you the time of hunting all over the island for them! GILL Codes 7, 8 and 9 give you an extra 3 minutes to do your exploring on each episode. If that's not enough, try GILL Code 10 for infinite time!

GILL CODE	KEY IN . . .	EFFECT . . .	
1	PAXSEIZE	Start with 9 ropes	
2	PAXSEIZA	Start with 1 rope	
3	SZSUAUVK	Infinite rope	
4	PAXIUIZE	Start with 9 units of food	
5	PAXIUIZA	Start with 1 unit of food	
6	SZXUIUVK	Infinite supply of food	
7	LANNLXPE	More time for Episode 1	
8	IANNGXLE	More time for Episode 2	
9	GPNNIZLP	More time for Episode 3	
10	SZENLZVG	Infinite time	
11	PAVSXGAA + GZVSUGSA	Start on Episode 2	
12	ZAVSXGAA + GZVSUGSA	Start on Episode 3	

Remember that you can pick'n'mix your codes.

Gilligan's Island is a trademark of Bandai America, Inc.

Some codes may cause undesired effects (which are not permanent). If this occurs,

Godzilla™ Game

Check out ZILLA Code 3—it's excellent! Or try ZILLA Code 2—it lets your power bar zoom back up to full as soon as it's been used. For a much harder game, go for ZILLA Code 4.

ZILLA CODE	KEY IN...	EFFECT...	
1	AEUSLKNY	Both monsters never lose power	
2	AEKSAGPE	Both monsters' power replenishes more quickly	
3	AAXITSNY	Both monsters invincible!	
4	VYXITSNN	Enemy inflicts more damage to both monsters	

Remeber that you can always pick'n'mix codes. Enter up to THREE separate codes at one time.
Godzilla is a trademark of Toho Company, Ltd.

Golgo 13™: The Mafat Conspiracy™ Game

Here are some awesome codes for you to try against The Mafat Conspiracy™! MAFAT Code 1 provides an infinite supply of bullets. MAFAT Codes 7, 8 and 9 each protect you from different dangers. If used together, they can make you totally invincible!

MAFAT CODE	KEY IN...	EFFECT...	
1	GXOGZZVG	Infinite bullets	
2	IASGUSZA	Fewer bullets picked up	
3	GPSGUSZA	More bullets picked up	
4	XTNIVXXK	Stop timer	
5	AYNIEXGL + AYVISXGL	Slower timer	
6	AZNIEXGL	Faster timer	
7	GZNGOTOY	Immune to physical damage	
8	GZOKSSON	Immune to weapon damage	
9	GXNGPOSN	Immune to damage in maze	

Remember that you can pick'n'mix your codes.
Golgo 13 and The Mafat Conspiracy are trademarks of Vic Tokai, Inc.

Golgo 13™—Top Secret Episode™ Game

To help our superspy along, we have a bunch of codes to stop him from taking any damage (GOL Codes 3 thru 5), as well as one to stop the superspy's energy level from going down (GOL Code 1). Perhaps the most interesting, however, is GOL Code 6, which gives your life force and bullet supply a super boost.

GOL CODE	KEY IN...	EFFECT...	
1	SXKVXAVG	Stop energy counting down	
2	GXUVXTSA	Doesn't use bullets in horizontal mode	
3	GXKNNPSA	Won't take damage in horizontal mode	
4	GZOEGGST	Won't take damage in pan/zoom mode	
5	GZKLZGST	Won't take damage in maze	
6	ZAVKIAAA	Gives life and bullets a super-boost	

Remember that you can pick'n'mix your codes! Up to three separate codes can be entered at one time.

Golgo 13 and Top Secret Episode are trademarks of Vic Tokai, Inc.

Goonies II™ Game

Here we have a few codes to give the last free Goonie™ a helping hand with lives. You can choose a more difficult game with only one life (GOON Code 2) or go further into the game with infinite lives from GOON Code 1. GOON Code 8 makes sure that you always have mega-jump, and GOON Code 10 gives you the super speed to outrun those bombs before they explode!

GOON CODE	KEY IN...	EFFECT...	
1	SZUGUYVG	Infinite lives	
2	PAXSZGLA	Start with 1 life	
3	TAXSZGLA	Start with 6 lives	
4	PAXSZGLE	Start with 9 lives	
5	GAUIZGZA + AGUIYGAZ	Start with 4 energy cells	
6	AAUIZGZE + EAUIYGAZ	Start with 8 energy cells	
7	IAVIAGPA	Start with boomerang	
8	LEUAOPZA	Always have mega-jump	
9	IEUEKPGA	Better jumping boots on pick-up	
10	ZESAPAPA	Super speed	
11	SXUASSVK	Infinite bombs on pick-up	
12	SZVAESVK	Infinite molotov bombs on pick-up	
13	SZNEEVVK	Infinite shots for sling on pick-up	

Remember that you can pick'n'mix your codes! You can enter up to THREE separate codes at one time, or one double-code (like GOON Code 6) and one single code (like GOON Code 4).

Goonies II and Goonie are trademarks of of Warner Bros, Inc. Used by Konami Industry Co. Ltd. under license

Gotcha!™ The Sport!™ Game

As well as codes to make this game easier, we also have one to make it harder. Try GOT Code 4 to give you less time to finish in—it's a real challenge. Alternatively, you could start with a double ration of ammo (GOT Code 2) . . . it's a good way to practice.

GOT CODE	KEY IN...	EFFECT...	
1	AASUTIPA	Freeze timer	
2	ZAEOKAPA	Start with double rations of ammo	
3	IAEPOAGA + PAEPVAIE	Increase timer to 59 seconds	
4	ZAEPOAGA + IAEPVAIA	Decrease timer to 25 seconds	

Remember that you can pick'n'mix your codes—you could start with twice as much ammunition and 59 seconds on the timer if you use GOT Codes 3 and 2 together.

Gotcha and The Sport are trademarks of Universal City Studios, Inc. Used by LJN Toys, Ltd., under license

Gradius™ Game

In this game, your firepower can be built up to awesome strength, but you always have to start again when you lose a life. Well, not anymore! GRAD Code 2 makes sure that you always keep

Some codes may cause undesired effects (which are not permanent). If this occurs,

all your weapons between lives. GRAD Code 6 makes sure that your power-capsule counter is preserved between lives, instead of resetting to the beginning. Check out GRAD Code 7 as well!

GRAD

CODE	KEY IN ...	EFFECT ...	
1	SXOOYYVI	Both players have infinite lives	
2	YGUONUZS + YGKPUUIL	Never lose weapons	
3	AENELZLA	Both players start with 1 life	
4	IENELZLA	Both players start with 6 lives	
5	AENELZLE	Both players start with 9 lives	
6	KOXOLYSP	Keep power capsules	
7	NNOEKPIE	Increase force field protection	

Remember that you can pick'n'mix your codes.

Gradius is a trademark of Konami Industry Co., Ltd.

The Guardian Legend™ Game

GUARD Code 1 gives you infinite energy to make you almost invincible! GUARD Code 4 gives you infinite shooting power. And GUARD Codes 6 thru 10 let you start on ANY level.

GUARD

CODE	KEY IN ...	EFFECT ...	
1	AAXTIUNY	Infinite energy	
2	AXVAIAAG	Start with less energy	
3	EEVAIAAG	Start with more energy	
4	GXOAKLST	Never use up shots	
5	OVOAKLSV + PEOASLAP	Use up minimum shots	
6	PAKVELAA	Start on area 1	
7	LAKVELAA	Start on area 3	
8	IAKVELAA	Start on area 5	
9	YAKVELAA	Start on area 7	
10	PAKVELAE	Start on area 9	

Remember that you can pick'n'mix codes. You can enter up to THREE separate codes at one time or one double code (Guard Code 5) and one single code (like Guard Code 1).

The Guardian Legend is a trademark of Irem Corp.

Guerilla War™ Game

There are a range of Game Genie™ codes to change the difficulty of this game. Why not try your skill by starting with a few more lives rather than using WAR Code 1 immediately?

WAR

CODE	KEY IN ...	EFFECT ...	
1	SLTKOV	Both players have infinite lives	
2	AELGVP	Both players start with 1 life	
3	IELGVP	Both players start with 6 lives	
4	PELGVO	Both players start with 9 lives	

Guerilla War is a trademark of SNK Corp. of America.
Game Genie is a trademark of Lewis Galoob Toys, Inc.

Gumshoe™ Game

We have a large variety of codes to enable you to change the playability of this game—you can vary the amount of bullets you start with, as well as how many lives you have. You can also change the timer value to give you extra time using GUM Code 10.

GUM CODE	KEY IN . . .	EFFECT . . .	
1	PAUENALA	Start with 1 life	
2	TAUENALA	Start with 6 lives	
3	PAUENALE	Start with 9 lives	
4	IZSEEAAI	Start with 25 bullets	
5	PASEKAAA	Start with 150 bullets	
6	ZASEKAAA	Start with 250 bullets	
7	PASAUALA	Gain 1 bullet on pick-up	
8	TASAUALA	Gain 6 bullets on pick-up	
9	LAKEGYTA	Timer set to 04:00	
10	PAKEGYTE	Timer set to 10:00	
11	SAKAVEKE	Different attack waves	

Remember, you can program your own codes! GUM Codes 1 through 3, 4 through 6, 9 and 10 might make good codes to try your programming luck on!

Gumshoe is a trademark of Nintendo of America Inc.

Gyromite™ Game

You can have more time to complete this game (GYRO Code 2) as well as being able to vary the amount of lives you start with—between one life (GYRO Code 3) and infinite lives (GYRO Code 1), which can change the playability of the game quite a bit.

GYRO CODE	KEY IN . . .	EFFECT . . .	
1	SUZAAI	Infinite lives	
2	ZEAAUS	Slow down timer	
3	PEUAGLIA	Start with 1 life	
4	ZEUAGLIE	Start with 10 lives	
5	GOUAGLIA	Start with 20 lives	

Remember that you can pick'n'mix your codes—you could try using GYRO Code 2 along with any of the other codes to make the game easier.

Gyromite is a trademark of Nintendo of America Inc.

Gyruss™ Game

Lots of useful codes for this mega-game! RUSS Code 2 makes sure that you never lose your twin-shot capability, while RUSS Codes 9 thru 11 let you start the game with some nice heavy weaponry. Take a shot at tuning the game to your preference with a couple of these Game Genie™ gems . . .

RUSS CODE	KEY IN . . .	EFFECT . . .	
1	AEEOIEZA	Infinite lives	

Some codes may cause undesired effects (which are not permanent). If this occurs,

2	GEEPIAZA + OEEPYAPA	Never lose twin shots
3	PAXEGLGA	Start with 1 ship
4	ZAXEGLGE	Start with 10 ships
5	GAKEATPA	Start with 4 phasers
6	AAKEATPE	Start with 8 phasers
7	ZEEPYAPA	Gain 2 phasers when you die with none
8	GEEPYAPA	Gain 4 phasers when you die with none
9	OAKEATPA	Start with twin shots + 1 phaser
10	KAKEATPA	Start with twin shots + 4 phasers
11	EAKEATPE	Start with twin shots + 8 phasers

Remember that you can pick'n'mix your codes! You can enter up to THREE separate codes at one time, or one double-code (like RUSS Code 2) and one single code (like RUSS Code 8).

Gyruss is a trademark of Konami Industry Co., Ltd.
Game Genie is a trademark of Lewis Galoob Toys, Inc.

Heavy Barrel™ Game

Have we got some excellent codes for you! Auto-Blasting power is yours with BAR Codes 1 and 2. Meanwhile, BAR Code 7 will help the young and inexperienced in their battle against the terrorists. Also, be sure to check out BAR Code 8 for invisibility and invincibility—its a BLAST! To activate Code 8 you will need to lose a life on each level.

BAR CODE	KEY IN . . .	EFFECT . . .
1	ENSTPVSN	Autofire for player 1
2	EYNVINSN	Autofire for player 2
3	AEKVXLII	Hand weapons last 4 times longer
4	ZAOVEPAA	Only 1 hand weapon
5	ENVVKLEI	Infinite hand weapons on pick-up for players 1 and 2
6	OXVVVLVS	Infinite hand weapons and firearms on pick-up for players 1 and 2
7	XVKZVEXK	Enemies don't fire handguns
8	XTOVVEXK	Become invisible and invincible!

Remember that you can pick'n'mix your codes. Enter up to THREE separate codes at one time.
Heavy Barrel is a trademark of Data East USA, Inc.

Heavy Shreddin'™ Game

Some great codes here to give you plenty of extra help. With SHRED Code 2 you're allowed infinite penalties, SHRED Code 1 slows down the timer, and SHRED Code 6 gives you much faster left and right movement. And if you're dying to see some of those later courses, check out SHRED Code 7—and use the 'A' button to select ANY level!

SHRED

CODE	KEY IN . . .	EFFECT . . .	
1	AUEXNVAO	Slow timer	
2	SXSOYIVG + SXOPPLVG + SXUOZLVG	Infinite penalties	
3	PEKAPLGA	1 penalty	
4	AEKAPLGE	8 penalties	
5	AOKAPLGA	16 penalties	
6	ZESEKLPA + ZEVEKLPA	Faster left and right movement	
7	NNUEYLAE	Select any level	

Heavy Shreddin' is a trademark of Parker Brothers.

Hudson's Adventure Island™ Game

Some extra lives can be really useful in this enormously popular game . . .You can also try one of the mega-jump codes (AI Code 8 thru 10) to add a bit of excitement. Maybe most important, though, is AI Code 7, which makes sure that you never lose weapons when you lose a life!

AI

CODE	KEY IN . . .	EFFECT . . .	
1	PEEEPALA	Start with 1 life	
2	TEEEPALA	Start with 6 lives	
3	PEEEPALE	Start with 9 lives	
4	SZOEGPVG	Start with infinite lives	
5	SXKKIAVG	Stop energy bar counting down	
6	GXNGLAKA	Become immune to rocks	
7	GZXEAPSA	Keep weapons	
8	SPEEIIEG	Can mega jump while at rest	
9	SPEETSOZ	Can mega jump while running	
10	AAEAYIPA + AEVEZGPZ	Multi-mega-maxi-moonjumps!	
11	AEKAPIPA + PEEEZIAA	Weird . . . Hudson™ can moonwalk!	

Remember that you can pick'n'mix your codes! You can enter up to THREE separate codes at one time, or one double-code (like AI Code 10) and one single code (like AI Code 4).

Hudson's Adventure Island and Hudson are trademarks of Hudson Soft USA, Inc.

The Hunt for Red October™ Game

As you can see, there are plenty of great codes to choose from here. Build up your defenses with RED Codes 12 or 13, maximimize your attack force with extra torpedoes using RED Codes 5 thru 10. Why not grab a few extra lives with Red Code 2? With all this help, you should be cruising into American waters pretty soon now!

RED

CODE	KEY IN. . .	EFFECT. . .	
1	PEVLYAIA	Start with 1 life	
2	ZEVLYAIE	Start with 10 lives	
3	SXEZXZVG	Infinite lives	

Some codes may cause undesired effects (which are not permanent). If this occurs,

4	SXEUPUVK	Infinite time
5	ZANLVKPO	Start with 10 horizontal torpedoes
6	ZLNLVKPP	Start with 50 horizontal torpedoes
7	LTNLVKPP	Start with 99 horizontal torpedoes
8	IANUUKYA	Start with 5 vertical torpedoes
9	ZLNUUKYA	Start with 50 vertical torpedoes
10	LTNUUKYA	Start with 99 vertical torpedoes
11	IEELSKZA	Start with 5 caterpillars
12	ZUELSKZA	Start with 50 caterpillars
13	LVELSKZA	Start with 99 caterpillars
14	IEEUXKZA	Start with 5 ECM's
15	ZUEUXKZA	Start with 50 ECM's
16	LVEUXKZA	Start with 99 ECM's
17	SXUXYSVK	Infinite horizontal torpedoes
18	SZUZPVVK	Infinite vertical torpedoes
19	OZEUEKOK + AAEUVGPA	Gain maximum power horizontal torpedoes on pick-up
20	OZSLNKOK + AASUSGPA	Gain maximum power vertical torpedoes, on pick-up

Remember that you can pick'n'mix your codes.

The Hunt For Red October is a trademark of Paramount Pictures.

Hydlide™ Game

Your strength, life and magic are usually low when you start this game. Not any more! LIDE Code 1 will give them a boost, and LIDE Code 2 will set them to full capacity! You can also heal rapidly using LIDE Codes 4 and 5. LIDE Code 3 is especially useful if you want to go on a mapping expedition—most monsters can't hurt you.

LIDE CODE	KEY IN . . .	EFFECT . . .	
1	AZKAAVZE	Boost strength, life, magic	
2	GTKAAVZA	Super boost strength, life, magic	
3	SXSGYYSA	Don't take damage from most monsters	
4	AEUEKVIA	Rapid healing	
5	AANOVZZA	Rapid magic healing	

Hydlide is a trademark of T&Esoft. Used by Fujisankei Communications International, Inc., under license

Ice Climber™ Game

There are some good codes for making your Ice Climber™ move faster, as well as one that makes you invincible (ICE Code 2). ICE Code 8 gives your little friend some amazing power jumping boots—try it and see!

ICE
CODE KEY IN . . .   EFFECT . . .

1   OKEIPGVS   Infinite lives

2   ATKSALAZ   Become invincible

3   AEXKTGLA   Start with 1 life
4   IEXKTGLA   Start with 6 lives
5   AEXKTGLE   Start with 9 lives

6   VNSKXUNN + ZESKULPA   Players double speed
7   SNSKXUNN + LESKULPA   Players triple speed

8   GPUKOAZX   Super jumping power

9   ELKITLEY   Monsters bump you
                                          instead of killing you

Remember that you can pick'n'mix your codes!
Ice Climber is a trademark of Nintendo of America Inc.

Ikari Warriors™ Game

There are a good selection of Game Genie™ codes for Ikari Warriors™—you can start the game
with infinite ammunition using IK Codes 2 thru 4, or a different number of lives (see IK Codes 5
thru 7). Of course, there is also an infinite lives code (IK Code 1) for those who need it.

IK
CODE KEY IN . . .   EFFECT . . .

1   SXSNZTVI   Infinite lives

2   SXXNVUVS   Infinite missiles for tank
3   SZONZSVS   Infinite bullets
4   SXEYZSVS   Infinite grenades

5   PAUYPTLA   Start with 1 life
6   TAUYPTLA   Start with 6 lives
7   PAUYPTLE   Start with 9 lives

8   ZUNNLZLT   Start with 50 bullets
9   LTEYALZL   Start with 99 grenades
10   PPEYALZU   Start with 25 grenades

Remember, you can program your own codes! IK Codes 5 through 7 and 8 through 10 might
make good codes to try your programming luck on!
Ikari Warriors is a trademark of SNK Corp. of America.
Game Genie is a trademark of Lewis Galoob Toys, Inc.

Ikari Warriors™ II: Victory Road™ Game

Paul™ and Vince™ can now be even more powerful and stand a much better chance of beating
Zang Zip the War Dog™ now that they have Game Genie™ on their side. If, however, you're
already absolutely brilliant at the game, then try using VICT Code 3 and see how far you get!

VICT
CODE KEY IN . . .   EFFECT . . .

1   OZUXVEPV + GAUXNAPA   Maximum power
                                          weapons on pick-up

74   *Some codes may cause undesired effects (which are not permanent). If this occurs,*

| 2 | GXOLYLST | Don't take damage from most enemies | |
| 3 | AUNYIYAT | Start game with half normal energy | |

Remember that you can pick'n'mix your codes!

Ikari Warriors, Victory Road, Paul, Vince and Zang Zip the War Dog are trademarks of SNK Corp. of America.
Game Genie is a trademark of Lewis Galoob Toys, Inc.

Imagefight™ Game

We have all the usual codes for lives, plus a whole bunch for level warps—IMAGE Codes 5 thru 8 for the Combat Simulation stages, and IMAGE Codes 9 and 10 for Real Combat. You can even choose which weapon you start with by using IMAGE Codes 12 thru 16!

IMAGE CODE	KEY IN . . .	EFFECT . . .	
1	SXSZTPVG	Infinite lives—both players	
2	PAVXLPLA	Start with 1 life—both players	
3	TAVXLPLA	Start with 6 lives—both players	
4	PAVXLPLE	Start with 9 lives—both players	
5	PAVZLPAA	Start at Combat Simulation Stage 2	
6	ZAVZLPAA	Start at Combat Simulation Stage 3	
7	LAVZLPAA	Start at Combat Simulation Stage 4	
8	GAVZLPAA	Start at Combat Simulation Stage 5	
9	IAVZLPAA	Start at Real Combat—1st Target	
10	TAVZLPAA	Start at Real Combat—2nd Target	
11	ATSLTKOZ	Never lose Pods	
12	PAELGGAA	Start with V Cannon	
13	ZAELGGAA	Start with Reflecting Ball	
14	LAELGGAA	Start with Drilling Laser	
15	GAELGGAA	Start with Seeking Missile	
16	IAELGGAA	Start with Seeking Laser	

Remember that you can pick'n'mix your codes. Enter up to THREE separate codes at one time.
Imagefight is a trademark of IREM America Corp.

The Immortal™ Game

For The Immortal™ we have codes that affect your energy and fatigue levels, as well as MORT Code 7, which increases the power of fireballs. MORT Code 1 keeps your enemy from regaining his strength and he becomes slower and a lot easier to defeat. MORT Code 5 stops you from losing energy in battles—now you'll be able to tackle any opponent!

MORT CODE	KEY IN . . .	EFFECT . . .	
1	GZOLIXVK	Enemy's fatigue level doesn't go down	
2	GZOUIXVK	Your fatigue level doesn't go down	
3	YLEUIXYN	Your fatigue level goes down faster	
4	NYEUIXYN	Your fatigue level goes down slower	
5	SZSLTXVK	Don't lose energy from fighting!	

refer to pages 10 and 11 for instructions. If you still have problems, call 1-513-868-8835.

75

| 6 | SZNLPXVV | Your fatigue level never rises |
| 7 | ZAKSIYPA | More damage from fireballs |

Remember that you can pick'n'mix your codes. You can enter up to THREE separate codes at one time.

The Immortal is a trademark of Electronic Arts.

Indiana Jones and the Temple of Doom™ Game

Indy™ can do so much with his fedora hat and his trusty bullwhip, but just think what he could do if he always had a sword and a gun! Just use INDY Codes 5 and 6 to make sure he always keeps these. Looking down the list you can see a big stack of level warps, as well as INDY Codes to change the number of lives and freeze the timer . . . go get those Thugees™!

INDY CODE	KEY IN . . .	EFFECT . . .	
1	SZEXOKVK	Infinite lives	
2	AEKLULGA	Start with 1 life	
3	PEKLULGE	Start with 10 lives	
4	TEKLULGE	Start with 15 lives	
5	SZSZGUVK	Always keep sword	
6	SZUXZVVK	Always keep gun	
7	SZXZAEVK	Freeze timer	
8	GLKUXGLV + LVEXUUGL + LTOXVKGL	Start with less time	
9	PPKLEKYA	Start on level 2	
10	IPKLEKYA	Start on level 4	
11	PPKLEKYE	Start on level 6	
12	IPKLEKYE	Start on level 8	

Remember, you can program your own codes! INDY Codes 2 through 4 might make good codes to try your programming luck on!

Indiana Jones and the Temple of Doom, Indy and Thugees are trademarks of Lucasfilm Ltd. Used by Mindscape Inc. under license.

Infiltrator™ Game

Never fear, Game Genie™ is here—to help Captain Jonny™ save the world! TRATOR Codes 6 thru 9 keep those vital weapons, and TRATOR Code 10 gives you unlimited time to complete your mission. If you think you're good enough, try TRATOR Codes 2 and 4. But if you think you could finish it with your eyes closed, try TRATOR Codes 3, 5 and 11 for a REALLY hard game!

TRATOR CODE	KEY IN . . .	EFFECT . . .	
1	ZPSLPXZA	Start with more Grenades	
2	IASLPXZA	Start with fewer Grenades	
3	AASLPXZA	Start with no Grenades	
4	LPKUIZTZ	Start with less Spray	
5	AAKUIZTZ	Start with no Spray	

Some codes may cause undesired effects (which are not permanent). If this occurs,

6	SXKXXIVG	Never lose Grenades outside buildings	
7	SZVKAIVG	Never lose Grenades inside buildings	
8	SXUXKIVG	Never lose Spray outside buildings	
9	SZUKYIVG	Never lose Spray inside buildings	
10	SZKLIKVK	Stop timer	
11	ILOULXPL	Start with less time	

Infiltrator and Captain Jonny are trademarks of Gray Matter. Licensed to Mindscape Inc.
Game Genie is a trademark of Lewis Galoob Toys, Inc.

Iron Tank™ Game

We've managed to come up with a code for Iron Tank™ that gives you a super-strong tank . . . be careful though, because you aren't totally invincible, and some of the heavier enemies can still make sure that you don't have a nice day.

TANK CODE	KEY IN . . .	EFFECT . . .	
1	OIOGIIPA + SXUKTKVK	Infinite lives	
2	OIOGIIPA + AAUKGGZA	Start with 1 life	
3	OIOGIIPA + IAUKGGZA	Start with 6 lives	
4	OIOGIIPA + AAUKGGZE	Start with 9 lives	
5	SLUVKESO	Super strong tank	

Remember that you can pick'n'mix your codes—you might want to try TANK Code 5 along with one of the other TANK Codes to let you explore the possibilities of the game.
Iron Tank is a trademark of SNK Corp. of America.

IronSword™—Wizards & Warriors™ II Game

The really notable codes for this game are IRON Code 11 and IRON Code 12, which give you permanent fleet-foot jumping and running powers—now that really is something! This game is really vast, so why not go exploring using any of the first three IRON Codes?

IRON CODE	KEY IN . . .	EFFECT . . .	
1	OXXANAVK	Infinite lives	
2	OZUAXPVK	Infinite continues	
3	GXXSNKVS	Infinite spells	
4	PENAEZLA + PESEXPLA	Start with 1 life	
5	TENAEZLA + TESEXPLA	Start with 6 lives	
6	AEEOEAZA	Food gives full energy	
7	AAOPNPZA	Drink gives full energy	
8	LEVEXZAA	Start with axe and helm	
9	ZEVAVXNY	Start with shield	
10	AAOAGUGA	Start with ironsword	
11	AASIYPLA	Fleet foot jumping	
12	OXKSYUPX	Fleet foot running	

refer to pages 10 and 11 for instructions. If you still have problems, call 1-513-868-8835.

13	LEEEPZAE	Start on wind level
14	GOEEPZAA	Start on tree level
15	TOEEPZAA	Start on water level
16	IOEEPZAA	Start on outer fire level
17	LUEEPZAA	Start on lower earth level
18	PUEEPZAA	Start on lower icefire mountain

Remember that you can pick'n'mix your codes! You can enter up to THREE separate codes at one time, or one double-code (like IRON Code 5) and one other code (like IRON Code 12).

IronSword and Wizards & Warriors are trademarks of Acclaim Entertainment Inc.

Isolated Warrior™ Game

It's up to you to stop the invading aliens from destroying your world, but you're not alone! We have the usual batch of cool Codes, such as ISO Codes 1 thru 4. Also, ISO Codes 5 thru 7 will make you a force to be reckoned with.

ISO CODE	KEY IN. . .	EFFECT. . .
1	PAXTIZLA	1 life
2	TAXTIZLA	6 lives
3	PAXTIZLE	9 lives
4	SZUVPAVG	Infinite lives
5	SZXOXSVK	Infinite bombs
6	AASVTXPA	Start with maximum energy and bombs
7	TEOAAYZA	More energy restored on pick-up
8	PEOAAYZA	Less energy restored on pick-up
9	PANEGAAA + VANEYESE + VEEAZESE	Start on Scene 2
10	ZANEGAAA + VANEYESE + VEEAZESE	Start on Scene 3
11	LANEGAAA + VANEYESE + VEEAZESE	Start on Scene 4
12	GANEGAAA + VANEYESE + VEEAZESE	Start on Scene 5
13	IANEGAAA + VANEYESE + VEEAZESE	Start on Scene 6

Remember that you can pick'n'mix your codes.

Isolated Warrior is a trademark of NTVIC.

Ivan "Ironman" Stewart's Super Off-Road™ Game

Off-road racing fans, check it out! OFF code 4 gives you infinite nitros—you may even be able to finish the game! If you're a pro driver already, try OFF Code 2 to improve the computer driver for a mega-challenge. Go for it!

OFF CODE	KEY IN . . .	EFFECT . . .
1	AAUEIEPP	Computer starts with no nitro boosts
2	ZLUEIEPP	Computer starts with double nitro boosts
3	ZLEVZSPP	Players start with double nitro boosts

Some codes may cause undesired effects (which are not permanent). If this occurs,

4	AEKISPPA	Players have infinite nitro boosts
5	PENTYGLA	Players have only 1 life
6	GGUTGGOU + GGUTIGAV + KTUTTKAL	Infinite money
7	TEKTYGAA	Lots of money and full equipment

Remember that you can pick'n'mix codes.

Ivan "Ironman" Stewart's Super Off-Road is a trademark of The Leland Corporation. Used under license by Tradewest, Inc.

Jackal™ Game

Again we have some really useful codes that all serious gamers will appreciate—you can keep all your weapons after dying using JACK Code 4, while JACK Code 5 causes you to reincarnate with a full array of weapons!

JACK CODE	KEY IN . . .	EFFECT . . .
1	SZPTSI	Both players have infinite lives
2	PAPKXZ	Both players start with 1 life
3	PAPKXX	Both players start with 9 lives
4	GXZTSG	Keep weapons after death
5	LEZTKG	Full weapons after death

Remember that you can pick'n'mix your codes! You can enter up to THREE separate codes at one time.

Jackal is a trademark of Konami Inc.

Jaws™ Game

We have a whole ocean of Game Genie™ codes for helping you beat the big fish that everyone loves to hate! Use JAW Code 5 to make sure you never lose your shells, or JAW Code 2 to give you infinite shells. There's also a bunch of others as well—try 'em and see!

JAW CODE	KEY IN . . .	EFFECT . . .
1	SZSATSVK	Infinite lives
2	SZVEYNSE	Infinite shells
3	PEOAGZLA	Start with 1 life
4	TEOAGZLA	Start with double lives
5	SZSELSTK	Don't lose shells on dying
6	SZSETSVK	Don't lose power on dying

Remember that you can pick'n'mix your codes! You can enter up to THREE separate codes at one time.

Jaws is a trademark of Universal City Studios, Inc. Used by LJN Toys, Ltd., under license.
Game Genie is a trademark of Lewis Galoob Toys, Inc.

Journey to Silius™ Game

Give yourself a head start in this battle against the 'intergalactic terrorists' with these excellent Game Genie™ codes! Pick out your best weapon from SILI Codes 8 thru 12. Protect yourself from enemy attacks with SILI Code 13. You can also go for mega-jump and super speed with SILI Codes 16 and 18.

SILI CODE	KEY IN ...	EFFECT ...	
1	SXNGYLVG	Infinite lives	
2	PAOSOTLA	Start with 1 life	
3	TAOSOTLA	Start with 6 lives	
4	PAOSOTLE	Start with 9 lives	
5	PEVIULLA	1 life after continue	
6	TEVIULLA	6 lives after continue	
7	PEVIULLE	9 lives after continue	
8	PEKSOGZA	Start with Machine Gun	
9	GEKSOGZA	Start with Laser Gun	
10	AEKSOGZE	Start with Homing Missiles	
11	AOKSOGZA	Start with Grenade Launcher	
12	IEKSOGZA	Start with Machine Gun & Laser Gun	
13	OTUVOZSV	Protection against most aliens	
14	AAXTKAZE	Some aliens are tougher	
15	PAXTKAZA	Some aliens are weaker	
16	TOOETOLA	Mega-jump	
17	AZVALPPA + EVNEYENY	Speed jump	
18	LPSEYPGA + KVNELEKN	Super speed	

Remember that you can pick'n'mix your codes.

Journey to Silius is a trademark of Sunsoft Corporation of America.
Game Genie is a trademark of Lewis Galoob Toys, Inc.

Joust™ Game

JOUS Code 4 is great—you get to fit a jet pack to the back of your bird and whizz around at turbo speed! JOUS Code 5 lets you start a new game at the last level reached in the last game, and we have the usual selection of codes to change the number of lives that you start with.

JOUS CODE	KEY IN ...	EFFECT ...	
1	SXXKKZVI	Infinite lives	
2	PEOGLAIA	Start with 1 life	
3	ZEOGLAIE	Start with 9 lives	
4	PASGKGAA	Turbo flying	
5	GXSKTASA + GXSKGASA + GXVGGASA	Start on last level reached	
6	GXVKOZSP	Heavens above?	

Some codes may cause undesired effects (which are not permanent). If this occurs,

Remember that you can pick'n'mix your codes!

Joust is a trademark of Williams Electronics Games, Inc. Used by HAL America, Inc., under license.

The Karate Kid™ Game

You've got to train hard to be The Karate Kid™! Check out the different stages with KARA Codes 10 thru 15. If you want to play with extra crane kicks, choose KARA Codes 7 or 8. It goes without saying that using KARA Codes 1, 2 and 3 gives you mega martial arts abilities!

KARA CODE	KEY IN . . .	EFFECT . . .	
1	SZOEKAVG	Infinite chances	
2	SXEXLYVG	Infinite crane kicks	
3	SZNXAYVG	Infinite drum punches on pick-up	
4	PENEZTLA	Start with 1 chance	
5	TENEZTLA	Start with 6 chances	
6	PENEZTLE	Start with 9 chances	
7	AAKVUGGE	8 crane kicks in 1-player game	
8	AAKVKGGE	8 crane kicks in 2-player game	
9	IAKVSGAA	Player 1 has 5 cranes in 'one on one'	
10	ZAKVVGPA	Start on stage 2, 1-player game	
11	ZAKVNGPA	Start on stage 2, 2-player game	
12	LAKVVGPA	Start on stage 3, 1-player game	
13	LAKVNGPA	Start on stage 3, 2-player game	
14	GAKVVGPA	Start on stage 4, 1-player game	
15	GAKVNGPA	Start on stage 4, 2-player game	

Remember that you can pick'n'mix your codes! You can enter up to THREE separate codes at one time.

The Karate Kid is a trademark of Columbia Pictures Industries, Inc. Used by LJN Toys, Ltd., under license.

Karnov™ Game

KARN Code 6 makes sure that you pick up three items at a time, instead of the usual one, while KARN Code 7 sees that you never lose most items when you use them. There are also a whole bunch of level warps to investigate (KARN Codes 8 thru 15).

KARN CODE	KEY IN . . .	EFFECT . . .	
1	SXKISXVK	Infinite lives	
2	GZVZNIVG	Freeze timer	
3	AAOSIAZA + AESIVTZA	Start with 1 life	
4	IAOSIAZA + IESIVTZA	Start with 6 lives	
5	AAOSIAZE + AESIVTZE	Start with 9 lives	
6	LEEGOYPA	Gain 3 of most items	
7	AEOKSYPA	Never lose most items	

8	PAUSAAAA	Start on stage 2
9	ZAUSAAAA	Start on stage 3
10	LAUSAAAA	Start on stage 4
11	GAUSAAAA	Start on stage 5
12	IAUSAAAA	Start on stage 6
13	TAUSAAAA	Start on stage 7
14	YAUSAAAA	Start on stage 8
15	AAUSAAAE	Start on stage 9

Karnov is a trademark of Data East USA, Inc.

Kickle Cubicle™ Game

KICK Code 1 gives you infinite lives. KICK Code 2 stops the timer so you can spend as long as you want on each level. And to start on the later levels, check out KICK Codes 5, 6 and 7. But watch out—some of them can be pretty tricky!

KICK
CODE	KEY IN . . .		EFFECT . . .	
1	SXEAATVG		Infinite lives	
2	SXNGSVVK		Stop timer	
3	YENKXVZA		Faster timer	
4	YENKXVZE		Slower timer	
5	GZKATXSE + GZUISOSE + PAUIOPAA		Start on land 2	
6	GZKATXSE + GZUISOSE + ZAUIOPAA		Start on land 3	
7	GZKATXSE + GZUISOSE + LAUIOPAA		Start on land 4	

Remember that you can pick'n'mix your codes.
Kickle Cubicle is a trademark of Irem America Corp.

Kid Icarus™ Game

Increase your spending power with KID Codes 2 thru 4! They'll give you more buying power in the shops, to help you get those special items!

KID
CODE	KEY IN . . .	EFFECT . . .	
1	OZETKISX	Change your energy!	
2	ZAKSXTPA	Small hearts worth 2 energy points	
3	IAKSXTPA	Small hearts worth 5 energy points	
4	GPKSSVZA	Big hearts worth 20 energy points	

Kid Icarus is a trademark of Nintendo of America Inc.

Kid Kool™ Game

Kid Kool™ fans out there will be pleased to see the KOOL Codes below. You can get some help with Codes 2 and 3, and if you want a bigger challenge try KOOL Codes 1 or 4!

KOOL
CODE	KEY IN . . .	EFFECT . . .	
1	PAVGIALA	Start with one life	
2	TAVGIALA	Start with double lives	
3	PAVGIALE	Start with triple lives	
4	PASKOILA	One life after continue	

Some codes may cause undesired effects (which are not permanent). If this occurs,

| 5 | SZKKXIVG | Infinite lives |
| 6 | VZOEOGVT | Stop the clock! |

You can pick 'n' mix your KOOL Codes—and remember, you can use up to three codes at once.
Kid Kool is a trademark of Vic Tokai Inc.

Kid Niki, Radical Ninja™ Game

Use NIKI Code 2 to give Kid Niki™ ninja jumping power! You can also freeze the timer if you want—just use NIKI Code 5. See also the comprehensive range of level warps available using NIKI Codes 7 thru 11. NOTE: These codes work on most Kid Niki cartridges.

NIKI
CODE   KEY IN . . .   EFFECT . . .

1	GXSOKIVG	Infinite lives	
2	NYUEXOEV	Ninja jumping power!	
3	PAOATZLA	Start with 1 life	
4	TAOATZLA	Start with 6 lives	
5	AESUEGPA	Freeze timer	
6	GAUELZTA + GEEPOTTA	Reduce timer value	
7	PEVAYPAA + PEUETPAA	Start on round 2	
8	ZEVAYPAA + ZEUETPAA	Start on round 3	
9	LEVAYPAA + LEUETPAA	Start on round 4	
10	GEVAYPAA + GEUETPAA	Start on round 5	
11	IEVAYPAA + IEUETPAA	Start on round 6	

Remember that you can pick'n'mix your codes! You can enter up to THREE separate codes at one time, or one double-code (like NIKI Code 11) and one single code (like NIKI Code 2).
Kid Niki, Radical Ninja and Kid Niki are trademarks of Data East USA, Inc.

King's Knight™ Game

Check out KING Codes 5, 6 and 7 to make sure that you have a super character in this amazing game! An accomplished King's Knight™ player can also make the game a bit more difficult by selecting KING Code 3, which gives you only a half measure of energy to play with!

KING
CODE   KEY IN . . .   EFFECT . . .

1	GZVXTPSA	Infinite energy	
2	AOSUAOGE	Start with double usual energy	
3	TESUAOGA	Start with half usual energy	
4	OTVXAPSV + PAVXPPAP	Only lose 1 energy point when hit	
5	PESUTPAA	Start with a better character	
6	ZESUTPAA	Start with the best character normally possible	
7	IESUTPAA	Start with a super character, better than normally possible	

King's Knight is a trademark of Square Soft, Inc.

Klax™ Game

Attention all Klax™ fans. We present the power to adjust the 'Drop Meter'! For a new challenge, check out KLAX Codes 1, 3 and 5, and try playing without being able to drop any tiles at all! Or else practice difficult things like 'The Big X' using KLAX Code 7. Have fun!

KLAX CODE	KEY IN . . .	EFFECT . . .
1	PAVESGLA	Start with 0 drops allowed
2	IAVESGLA	Start with 5 drops allowed
3	PANENGGA	When starting on level 6: 0 drops allowed
4	IANENGGA	When starting on level 6: 5 drops allowed
5	PEOAXGIA	When starting on level 11: 0 drops allowed
6	LEOAXGIA	When starting on level 11: 3 drops allowed
7	SXXLUGVT	Infinite drops!

Klax is a trademark of Atari Games Corp. Used by Tengen, Inc. under license.

Knight Rider™ Game

With RIDE Codes 2 and 3, you'll find that you can only continue once after using them. RIDE Codes 4 thru 6 give you infinite amounts of shields, missiles and lasers, and you can also change the number of lives you start with when you continue a game by using RIDE Codes 11 thru 13.

RIDE CODE	KEY IN . . .	EFFECT . . .
1	SXXEGEVK + SXKEIEVK	Infinite lives
2	AANKOAZA + VTNKSESE	Start with 1 life
3	IANKOAZA + VTNKSESE	Start with 6 lives
4	SZXSYTSA	Infinite shield
5	SZEXUNVK	Infinite missiles
6	GXXZSVVK	Infinite laser
7	SZKZYOSU + LYKXAOTT	Start with 99 missiles
8	SZSZLOSU + PYSZGPGN	Start with 99 lasers
9	SZUZAOSU + ATUZPPTV	Start with full gasoline
10	SZUXGOSU + ITUXIOZV	Start with full shield
11	AEVALAZA	Start with 1 life after continue
12	IEVALAZA	Start with 6 lives after continue
13	AEVALAZE	Start with 9 lives after continue

Remember, you can program your own codes! RIDE Codes 11 through 13 might make good codes to try your programming luck on!

Knight Rider is a trademark of Universal City Studios Inc. Used by Acclaim Entertainment, Inc., under license

Kung Fu™ Game

KUNG Code 7 gives one life to player 1, and three lives to player 2—just the thing when you're playing little bro or sis (or pee and em). KUNG Code 8 makes you stronger, so when the enemy grabs you, you can shrug them off quicker—before they do much damage! KUNG Codes 9, 10 and 11 all make fighting much harder. Are you Kung Fu™ experts up for it?

KUNG CODE	KEY IN . . .	EFFECT . . .
1	SUAAXA	Both players have infinite lives

Some codes may cause undesired effects (which are not permanent). If this occurs,

2	PEZELG	Both players have 1 life	
3	PEZELK	Both players have 9 lives	
4	GZVKIYSA + ATVKYNGG	Don't die when time runs out	
5	GZLATG	Player 1 start at last level reached	
6	GZLEPG	Player 2 start at last level reached	
7	SEZEGG	Give player 2 an advantage	
8	AEVXLSPT	Enemy easier to shrug off	
9	ZEVXPIGE	Enemy harder to shrug off	
10	LEEXSYPA	Normal enemies do more damage	
11	XYUXEUZK	Knife thrower harder to beat	

Remember that you can pick'n'mix your codes!
Kung Fu is a trademark of Irem Corp. Used by Nintendo of America Inc. under license.

Kung Fu Heroes™ Game

Little Jacky™ and Lee™ can certainly save the Princess Min-Min™ and her treasures—all they need is a little boost with these Game Genie™ codes. You can pick the number of lives you start with, choose how many power kicks you have, warp to any level and even have a couple of other goodies too—just look down the list, wazz a code or two into your Game Genie™ and get going!

HERO CODE	KEY IN . . .	EFFECT . . .	
1	AESLZLPA	Infinite lives	
2	PASXSPIA	Start with 1 life	
3	PASXSPIE	Start with 9 lives	
4	AEVSPAPA	Infinite miracle kicks	
5	GPVZXPAA	Start with 20 miracle kicks	
6	OZSZXPSX + GASZUOSG	Start on Castle 2	
7	OZSZXPSX + AASZUOSK	Start on Castle 3	
8	OZSZXPSX + GASZUOSK	Start on Castle 4	
9	OZSZXPSX + APSZUOSG	Start on Castle 5	
10	OZSZXPSX + GPSZUOSG	Start on Castle 6	
11	OZSZXPSX + APSZUOSK	Start on Castle 7	
12	OZSZXPSX + GPSZUOSK	Start on Castle 8	
13	PASZNPLA	Use with warp to start with 1 life	
14	TASZNPLA	Use with warp to start with 6 lives	
15	PASZNPLE	Use with warp to start with 9 lives	
16	ZAXUEGIA	2 E-balls for an extra man	

| 17 | GAOKOGPA + KYXGOKNN | Mega jumps left and right |

Remember that you can pick'n'mix your codes! You can enter up to THREE separate codes at one time, or one double-code (like HERO Code 12) and one other code (like HERO Code 13).
Kung Fu Heroes, Little Jacky, Lee and Princess Min-Min are trademarks of Culture Brain USA, Inc.
Game Genie is a trademark of Lewis Galoob Toys, Inc.

The Last Starfighter™ Game

Pro players of this mega-shoot'em up should check out LAST Code 1 for a harder game. If the two people playing are not evenly matched, LAST Code 4 provides a good handicap for player 1. World Warping fans, see LAST Codes 6 thru 8.

LAST CODE	KEY IN . . .	EFFECT . . .	
1	PANENLIA	Players 1 and 2 start with 1 life	
2	TANENLIA	Players 1 and 2 start with 6 lives	
3	PANENLIE	Players 1 and 2 start with 9 lives	
4	KEEAVLSA	Player 2 starts with 1 life	
5	SZVPATVG	Players 1 and 2 have infinite lives	
6	GAVEKLAA + GZVENLSA + GZNAOLSA	Player 1 start on level 5	
7	PAVEKLAE + GZVENLSA + GZNAOLSA	Player 1 start on level 10	
8	IAVEKLAE + GZVENLSA + GZNAOLSA	Player 1 start on level 14	
9	GXUPLGSA	Stop irritating shake	

The Last Starfighter is a trademark of Universal/Lorimar, a Joint Venture.

Legacy of the Wizard™ Game

You can pick your favorite characters in Legacy of the Wizard™ and give them a boost by using WIZ Codes 5 thru 12. There are also codes to make sure that you never lose items and never take any damage from monsters, as well as one which makes the shopkeeper forget to charge you when you buy things in the shop!

WIZ CODE	KEY IN . . .	EFFECT . . .	
1	GXNTYYVG	Infinite magic power	
2	GXSVLGVI	Never lose items	
3	GZKVUASA	Shopkeeper forgets to charge	
4	GXVTZYSA	Never take any damage	
5	LEUYKYPA	Lyll's™ strength tripled	
6	AUUYUNZP	Lyll's jumping improved	

Some codes may cause undesired effects (which are not permanent). If this occurs,

7	LEUYEYPA	Roas'™ strength tripled
8	ZXXNNYGO	Roas' jumping improved
9	PEXNEYLE	Xemn's™ strength tripled
10	AXXYNYZP	Xemn's jumping improved
11	TEXNKYZA	Menya's™ strength tripled
12	AXXNUYGP	Menya's jumping improved

Remember that you can pick'n'mix your codes! You can enter up to THREE separate codes at one time.

Legacy of the Wizard, Lyll, Roas, Xemn and Menya are trademarks of Broderbund Software, Inc.

The Legend of Kage™ Game

Be careful how you use the super-ninja-power jump ability (KAGE Code 3)—if you hit the top of the screen, you fall back and may be vulnerable to attack. Also, you can outrun even the swiftest enemies using KAGE Code 4 . . .try it!

KAGE CODE	KEY IN . . .	EFFECT . . .
1	SXVALZVG	Both players have infinite lives
2	KEOATAVA	Both players start with 28 lives
3	YAKXYPGE + YASZAPGE + YASZPPGE	Super-ninja-power jumping ability
4	GASAOLZA	Super-ninja-power running ability

Remember, you can program your own codes! KAGE Code 2 might make a good code to try your programming luck on!

The Legend of Kage is a trademark of Taito America Corporation.

The Legend of Zelda™ Game

Help Link™ save Zelda™ with these excellent Game Genie™ codes—at last you will be able to complete this epic adventure, destroy the evil Ganon,™ and rescue the Princess!

ZELD CODE	KEY IN . . .	EFFECT . . .
1	AVVLAUSZ	Don't take damage from anything
2	YYKPOYZZ	Create character with 8 life hearts
3	NYKPOYZX	Create character with 16 life hearts

The Legend of Zelda, Link, Zelda and Ganon are trademarks of Nintendo of America Inc.
Game Genie is a trademark of Lewis Galoob Toys, Inc.

Legendary Wings™ Game

Another brilliant game for which you can select a code to make sure that all weapons are kept between lives—try WING Code 1. You can also adjust the number of lives that player 1 starts with (WING Codes 2 thru 4), so you can play with a friend who isn't as good as you and still have fun!

WING CODE	KEY IN . . .	EFFECT . . .	
1	AAEEGLPA + AEEATIPA	Never lose weapons after death	
2	PEEALYLA	Player 1 starts with 1 life	
3	TEEALYLA	Player 1 starts with 6 lives	
4	PEEALYLE	Player 1 starts with 9 lives	
5	PANEAYLA	Both players start with 1 life	
6	TANEAYLA	Both players start with 6 lives	
7	PANEAYLE	Both players start with 9 lives	
8	ZANAIZPA + ZEVAPIPA	Gain double powers on pick-up	
9	LANAIZPA + ZEVAPZPA	Gain triple powers on pick-up	

Remember that you can pick'n'mix your codes!

Legendary Wings is a trademark of Capcom USA, Inc.

Life Force™ Game

Loadsa codes for Life Force™! We've got codes that start you off with special weapons, codes that give you extra lives, codes that warp you to new levels, and even codes that make losing a life seem not nearly so bad! Just scan down the list and pick out the LIFE Codes that you want to try most.

LIFE CODE	KEY IN . . .	EFFECT . . .	
1	GZKGILVI	Infinite lives	
2	PEKVNTLA	Start with 1 life	
3	TEKVNTLA	Start with 6 lives	
4	ULKGZGKG	Keep weapons after death	
5	GZSGLTSP	Keep pods after death	
6	PEKGPTAA	Start with Speed	
7	ZEKGPTAA	Start with Missile	
8	LEKGPTAA	Start with Ripple	
9	GEKGPTAA	Start with Laser	
10	IEKGPTAA	Start with Option	
11	TEKGPTAA	Start with Force Field	

Some codes may cause undesired effects (which are not permanent). If this occurs,

12	PEUTSTAA	Start at the volcanic stage
13	ZEUTSTAA	Start at the prominence stage
14	LEUTSTAA	Start at cell stage 2
15	GEUTSTAA	Start at the temple stage
16	IEUTSTAA	Start at the mechanical city stage

Life Force is a trademark of Konami Inc.

Little Nemo: The Dream Master™ Game

For Little Nemo™ we have codes for lives, jumping, running, energy and level warping! NEMO Code 5 makes your jumps extra high and NEMO Code 6 lets you do speed jumps without taking a run. For a turbo-boost, check out NEMO Code 7. There's also NEMO Code 8 to stop your life bar from running down, and NEMO Codes 9 thru 15 let you start on any level!

NEMO CODE	KEY IN . . .	EFFECT . . .
1	PEKKSZLA	1 life
2	TEKKSZLA	6 lives
3	PEKKSZLE	9 lives
4	SZOKSLVG	Infinite lives
5	TOKZKNZA	Mega-jump
6	GESLYPPA + UYUUIOVN	Speed jumps
7	ZEXLLPPA + SYEUPOVN	Super speed
8	SXKTGEVK	Infinite 'life'
9	PEUKOZAA	Start on stage 2
10	ZEUKOZAA	Start on stage 3
11	LEUKOZAA	Start on stage 4
12	GEUKOZAA	Start on stage 5
13	IEUKOZAA	Start on stage 6
14	TEUKOZAA	Start on stage 7
15	YEUKOZAA	Start on stage 8

Remember that you can pick'n'mix your codes.

Little Nemo: The Dream Master is a trademark of Capcom U.S.A., Inc.

Lode Runner™ Game

LODE Code 5 is useful—it increases the gravity around you, so that you can fall faster than the guards. Use LODE Code 2 carefully because it makes you completely invincible—you can walk thru the guards with no problem, but if you fall down a hole you won't be able to get out—press SELECT then START to restart on the same level.

LODE CODE	KEY IN . . .	EFFECT . . .
1	GZNGYIVG	Infinite lives
2	GXOKIGEY + GXOGTGEY + GZNGLGEY	Become invincible
3	PASKLTIA	Start with 1 life
4	ZASKLTIE	Start with 10 lives

| 5 | GAUGVGYA + AAKGEGGA | Heavy gravity |
| 6 | APOIGPAL | Moonwalk! |

Remember that you can pick'n'mix your codes! You might want to try LODE Code 4 and LODE Code 5 together for a very different game!

Lode Runner is a trademark of Broderbund Software, Inc.

Low G Man™ Game

LOW Code 7 provides infinite lives, which is ideal for exploring everything in this game! LOW Code 9 gives you infinite fuel. On a new life, LOW Code 12 gives you a super power weapon, and LOW Code 13 gives you full Anti-Gravity Jumping. LOW Codes 14 thru 17 will give you TEN of each weapon on pick-up!

LOW CODE	KEY IN . . .	EFFECT . . .	
1	PEXIZTLA	Start with 1 life	
2	TEXIZTLA	Start with 6 lives	
3	PEXIZTLE	Start with 9 lives	
4	PEOSKALA	1 life after continue	
5	TEOSKALA	6 lives after continue	
6	PEOSKALE	9 lives after continue	
7	SZNIEEVK	Infinite lives	
8	GZKINOVK	Stop timer	
9	SZVSKOVK	Vehicle fuel never runs out	
10	AAEZATZE	Full energy gained from capsules	
11	PAEZATZA	Less energy gained from capsules	
12	LAVSKAPA	Full EMDP on a new life	
13	ZAVIKAAA	Full AGM on a new life	
14	ZEOZZTLE	Pick up 10 boomerangs	
15	ZAVXGTLE	Pick up 10 fireballs	
16	ZEUXATLE	Pick up 10 bombs	
17	ZESXTTLE	Pick up 10 waves	

Remember that you can pick'n'mix your codes.

Low G Man is a trademark of Taxan USA Corporation.

Mad Max™ Game

Mad Max™ is all about the survival of the fittest, and these codes will make YOU fitter than the rest! You can adjust the amount of damage that you (or your car) will take by using MAX Codes 4 thru 9. An ammo boost will come in handy—check out MAX Code 3!

MAX CODE	KEY IN . . .	EFFECT . . .	
1	NYEYVYAX	Start with full food and water	
2	AGOYUYEA	Start with less ammo	
3	SXVAEVVK	Infinite ammo	

Some codes may cause undesired effects (which are not permanent). If this occurs,

4	AENEPYAP	No damage done to car
5	GENEPYAP	Less damage done to car
6	AXNEPYAP	More damage done to car
7	AAUAUEAA	No damage done to you
8	GAUAUEAA	Less damage done to you
9	APUAUEAA	More damage done to you
10	AVKVLPAZ	A better tune-up
11	GEEATZYA + GLKELZYL	Cheaper arena pass
12	AANEPZPA	Dynamite is free
13	AAVEGZPA	Ammo is free

Remember that you can pick'n'mix your codes.
Mad Max is a trademark of Warner Bros., Inc. Licensed to Mindscape Inc.

The Magic of Scheherazade™ Game

Now it is safe to enter the magical land of Scheherazade™ because Game Genie™ is here to grant you three wishes! MAGIC Code 5 will bring you great riches. MAGIC Codes 8 and 10 will allow you to keep your bread and Mashroobs™. And MAGIC Codes 1 thru 4 allow you to choose your number of lives.

MAGIC CODE	KEY IN . . .	EFFECT . . .
1	PAKTAZLA	1 life
2	TAKTAZLA	6 lives
3	PAKTAZLE	9 lives
4	SXEVPLVG	Infinite lives
5	VTXVIZSA	Start with 150 Gold Coins
6	ZAUTAZIA	Start with only 20 Gold Coins
7	POKAOZZU	Less energy gained from Bread
8	SXUEXXVK	Never lose Bread
9	ZAEEXGIA	Less magic gained from Mashroobs
10	SZEAEKVK	Never lose Mashroobs
11	OTSXLGSV	Infinite energy
12	OTSXLGSV + PASXGGAA	Take minimum damage

Remember, you can pick and mix your codes, so why not try out MAGIC Codes 4, 5 and 10 for an easier game?

The Magic of Scheherazade and Mashroobs are trademarks of Culture Brain USA, Inc.
Game Genie is a trademark of Lewis Galoob Toys, Inc.

refer to pages 10 and 11 for instructions. If you still have problems, call 1-513-868-8835.

91

MagMax™ Game

A whole host of life codes for MagMax™—you can practice with a lot of lives, then go to a friend's house and give him a beating! Oh—always remember to take your Game Genie™ with you when you visit friends—it'll work with their listed games too!

MAX CODE	KEY IN . . .	EFFECT . . .	
1	SZVVYTVG	Infinite lives in a 1-player game	
2	AEEVITPA	Both players have infinite lives in a 2-player game	
3	AEKGKLZA	Both players start with 1 life	
4	IEKGKLZA	Both players start with 6 lives	
5	AEKGKLZE	Both players start with 9 lives	

MagMax is a trademark of Nihon Bussan Co., Ltd. Used by Fujisankei Communications International, Inc., under license.
Game Genie is a trademark of Lewis Galoob Toys, Inc.

Mappy Land™ Game

Mappy™ usually starts the game with three toys—you can start with six if you use MAP Code 4. You can also combine this code with MAP Codes 6 thru 8 to start the game with other 'weapons' instead of toys.

MAP CODE	KEY IN . . .	EFFECT . . .	
1	SZKXITVG	Infinite lives	
2	AEXXTAZA	Start with 1 life	
3	IEXXTAZA	Start with 6 lives	
4	TESXALLA	Start with 6 toys	
5	PESXALLA	Start with 1 toy	
6	LESZALAA	Start with coins, not toys	
7	PESZALAA	Start with fish, not toys	
8	ZESZALAA	Start with pots, not toys	

Remember that you can pick'n'mix your codes—you might try using MAP Code 4 and MAP Code 7 together to start the game with 6 fish!

Mappy Land and Mappy are trademarks of Namco.

Mario Bros.™ Game

These guys have been around a long time—some of us remember seeing them first in Donkey Kong™ in the early Eighties! Anyway, we've got codes: BROS Codes 5 and 6 get them off and running faster, BROS Code 7 is great to mega-jump over tall pipes or onto some of those high blocks. And for a code with a twist, try BROS Code 10—the coins kill you! Ahhhhhhh!

BROS CODE	KEY IN . . .	EFFECT . . .	
1	SXTIEG	Infinite lives	
2	AAISPL	Start with 1 life	
3	IAISPL	Start with 6 lives	
4	AAISPU	Start with 9 lives	
5	PENGSAAA	Faster Mario™ & Luigi™	
6	ZENGSAAA	Mega fast Mario & Luigi	

Some codes may cause undesired effects (which are not permanent). If this occurs,

7	VYSYAUKY + VYSYPUKY	Mega-jumping Mario & Luigi	
8	EZEKEPKZ + ZAEKOPNG	Faster baddies	
9	EZEKEPKZ + LAEKOPNG	Mega fast baddies	
10	AEUIUGAG	Coins kill you!	

Mario Bros., Mario, Luigi, and Donkey Kong are trademarks of Nintendo of America Inc.

Mechanized Attack™ Game

Here we have it folks—extra lives, extra weapons and added protection to see you through the enemy assault. Also, lots of codes to reduce lives and weapons if you want a harder game. Be sure to play using MEC Codes 11 and 12 for infinite bullets and grenades—excellent fun!

MEC CODE	KEY IN . . .	EFFECT . . .	
1	SXUNPEVK	Infinite lives	
2	EZOKIAXZ + PAOKTAAA + KANKPEVE	Start with only 1 life	
3	EZOKIAXZ + TAOKTAAA + KANKPEVE	Start with 6 lives	
4	EZOKIAXZ + PAOKTAAE + KANKPEVE	Start with 9 lives	
5	AEVOAPLA	Reduce damage by half	
6	EZOKIAXZ + AAOKTAAA + KANKTEVE	Start with only 1 magazine	
7	EZOKIAXZ + YAOKTAAA + KANKTEVE	Start with 8 magazines	
8	GPONAOAZ + GPEYLEAZ	Magazine holds only half normal amount of bullets after first magazine used	
9	EZOKIAXZ + PAOKTAAA + KEEGZEVE	Start with only 1 grenade	
10	EZOKIAXZ + AAOKTAAE + KEEGZEVE	Start with 8 grenades	
11	SZUNTOVK	Infinite grenades	
12	SZEYIOVK	Infinite bullets	

Remember that you can pick'n'mix your codes.
Mechanized Attack is a trademark of SNK Corporation of America.

MegaMan™ Game

Help MegaMan™ defeat the evil Dr. Wily™ and his super villains! MEGA Code 9 gives MegaMan mega-jump . . . a great code! You can increase your chance of survival by using MEGA Code 7.

MEGA CODE	KEY IN . . .	EFFECT . . .	
1	OZSKPZVK	Infinite lives	
2	AASPLAZA	Start with 1 life	
3	IASPLAZA	Start with 6 lives	
4	AASPLAZE	Start with 9 lives	
5	SZKZGZSA	Infinite energy	
6	TAXOIOGO	Start with half energy	
7	AVVXLPSZ	No harm from any enemies, except super villains	

8	OXSLEEPV + AUSLOEAZ	Always get maximum points for shooting super villains	
9	TAOOYTGA	MegaMan mega-jump	

MegaMan and Dr. Wily are trademarks of Capcom USA, Inc.

MegaMan 2™ Game

Infinite lives and infinite energy can even be useful for a super hero like MegaMan™! Use MEGA Codes 1 and 2 to do this. Also, look at MEGA Codes 8 thru 10, which give you much improved jumping skills.
NOTE: all codes make the music sound strange. It's harmless. MEGA Code 2 may cause you to get "stuck" near the end of the game when your weapon energy runs out. If this happens, just reset and start again.

MEGA CODE	KEY IN . . .	EFFECT . . .
1	SXUGTPVG	Infinite lives
2	SXXTPSSE	Infinite energy
3	TEKAIEGO	Start with half energy
4	PANALALA	Start with 1 life
5	TANALALA	Start with 6 lives
6	PANALALE	Start with 9 lives
7	LZVSSZYZ	Gives burst-fire from normal weapon
8	TANAOZGA	Power jumps
9	AANAOZGE	Super power jumps
10	APNAOZGA	Mega power jumps
11	GZKEYLAL	Maximum weapon energy on pick-up
12	PGEAKOPX	Moonwalking

Remember that you can pick'n'mix your codes! You can enter up to three MEGA Codes into your Game Genie™ at one time!
MegaMan 2 and MegaMan are trademarks of Capcom USA, Inc.
Game Genie is a trademark of Lewis Galoob Toys, Inc.

MegaMan 3™ Game

Check out the radical codes for the awesome MegaMan3™. Give yourself some extra lives or go all the way with infinite lives! There's also infinite energy with MEGA Code 11, while MEGA Codes 9 and 10 come in handy for sliding out the way of the enemy. Also, be sure to try MEGA Codes 8, 12 and 13 for mega-jumping and super speed running.

MEGA CODE	KEY IN . . .	EFFECT . . .
1	AENKKAZA	1 life
2	IENKKAZA	6 lives
3	AENKKAZE	9 lives
4	PAOONPZA	1 life after continue
5	IAOONPZA	6 lives after continue
6	AAOONPZE	9 lives after continue
7	AEEGXLPA	Infinite lives

Some codes may cause undesired effects (which are not permanent). If this occurs,

8	YEUKOTGA	Mega-jumping MegaMan™	
9	ASXSTLGP	Longer slides	
10	NNKIALEE	Speedy slides	
11	GXVAAASA	Infinite energy	
12	NYKGXSGK	Faster MegaMan	
13	ZAKGNIPA	Mega fast MegaMan	

Remember that you can pick'n'mix your codes. You can enter up to three separate codes at one time.
MegaMan 3 and MegaMan are trademarks of Capcom USA.

Mendel Palace™ Game

MEND Code 5 gives player 1 a large advantage: he or she gets 10 lives, and player 2 only gets the normal 3 lives! MEND Code 7 also gives player 1 an advantage: he or she gets all of player 2's speed-ups. To earn yourself some extra lives and speed-ups, MEND Code 8 is great—it gives you five stars on every pick-up instead of just one!

MEND CODE	KEY IN . . .	EFFECT . . .	
1	SLSIXXVS	Infinite lives	
2	AAVZLPZA	1 life	
3	IAVZLPZA	5 lives	
4	AAVZLPZE	9 lives	
5	KEXLXKSE	Player 1 has more lives	
6	KEXLSKSE	Player 2 has more lives	
7	SZUIOOSU + VTUSEOVN	Player 1 gains player 2's speed-ups	
8	IEXIAIPA	Pick up more stars	

Mendel Palace is a trademark of Hudson Soft USA, Inc.

Metal Gear™ Game

Use GEAR Codes 5 and 6 if you want have a look around other strongholds without having to play through them, but be warned—it's is not an easy way to finish the game! You will miss important items that are found earlier. However, it's a great way to find out what the enemy is like at the different strongholds, and is good for practice.

GEAR CODE	KEY IN . . .	EFFECT . . .	
1	SZUYPZVG	Don't take hits from bullets	
2	SXVTXZVG	No hits taken in hand-to-hand fights with most enemies	
3	XZVSAYVZ + PAVSPNTT + AEKSZYIE	Start with an energy boost	
4	XZVSAYVZ + PAVSPNTT + GEKSZYIE	Start with a super energy boost	
5	ZASILYPA	Mystery location 1	
6	GASILYPA	Mystery location 2	

| 7 | EOSZUIEL | One to show your friends | |

Remember that you can pick'n'mix your codes!

Metal Gear is a trademark of Konami Industries Co. Ltd.

Metroid™ Game

Need some help to get thru to the Motherbrain™? You can increase your missile power using your Game Genie™ and MET Codes 3 and 4. Help in your fight against evil can also be had from MET Code 1, which makes sure that you always have some energy!

MET CODE	KEY IN . . .	EFFECT . . .	
1	SXSGNVSE	Minimum energy of 30	
2	SZUILUVK	Infinite rockets on pick-up	
3	ZENSXLIE	Gain 10 rockets on pick-up	
4	YENSXLIE	Gain 15 rockets on pick-up	
5	YAXGVPLA	Extra energy	

Remember, you can program your own codes! MET Codes 3 and 4 might make good codes to try your programming luck on!

Metroid and Motherbrain are trademarks of Nintendo of America Inc.
Game Genie is a trademark of Lewis Galoob Toys, Inc.

Mickey Mousecapade™ Game

You can get further into the game by using some of these handy Game Genie™ MICK Codes to give yourself extra lives, or even infinite energy (MICK Code 5)! You can also make sure that you get your shooting ability a little early—try MICK Code 6 on for size.

MICK CODE	KEY IN . . .	EFFECT . . .	
1	SZSOPZVG	Infinite lives	
2	PESOIPGA	Start with 2 lives	
3	IESOIPGA	Start with 6 lives	
4	AESOIPGE	Start with 9 lives	
5	OVOPPTSV	Infinite energy	
6	GPSIEVGE + LAVSVTZA	Mickey™ and Minnie™ can shoot on any level	

Remember that you can pick'n'mix your codes!

Mickey Mousecapade, Mickey and Minnie are trademarks of Walt Disney Company. Used by Capcom USA, Inc., under license.
Game Genie is a trademark of Lewis Galoob Toys, Inc.

Mighty Bomb Jack™ Game

JACK Code 11 lets you pass through walls—it even lets you HIDE in the walls if you want! With JACK Code 9 you can use your powers without using up power coins. Worried about the torture room? No problem. JACK Code 10 will totally disable it!

JACK CODE	KEY IN . . .	EFFECT . . .	
1	PAOEZZLA	1 life	
2	TAOEZZLA	6 lives	
3	PAOEZZLE	9 lives	

Some codes may cause undesired effects (which are not permanent). If this occurs,

4	VZUEZNVK	Infinite lives
5	AKOEGYAT	Less time in game
6	EEOEGYAT	More time in game
7	SXXALNVK	Stop timer
8	SXOESEVK	Enemies don't return from coin transformation
9	SZEEXUVK	Power coins are not used up
10	OESPNTLA	Disable torture room
11	ZEUOUAPA	Jump through walls

Remember to mix your favorite codes, like JACK Codes 10 and 11, and don't forget you can have three wishes!

Mighty Bomb Jack is a trademark of Tecmo, Ltd.

Mike Tyson's Punch Out™ Game

In this knockout game, you usually lose a heart whenever you miss a punch or if you get hit. But PUNCH Code 2 makes sure you never lose hearts and PUNCH Code 3 lets you keep your stars. For PUNCH Code 1, hold down your SELECT button between rounds to fully replenish your stamina! More championship codes include PUNCH Code 6, which increases the bonus energy you gain from hitting your opponent, and PUNCH Code 8, which gives your normal punch a punishing effect!

PUNCH CODE	KEY IN . . .	EFFECT . . .
1	KVKAAGLA	Refresh stamina totally between rounds
2	GZKETGST	Never lose hearts
3	ALNEVPEY	Never lose stars when punching or being punched
4	SZVAAOIV	Take less damage
5	SZVALPAX	Take even less damage
6	AGUELIGA	Energy replenishment
7	SZSELPAX	No energy replenishment for opponent
8	AAVETLGA	Normal punches do more damage
9	STNAPUIV	Stunned punches do less damage

Remember that you can pick'n'mix your codes! You could try using PUNCH Codes 1, 2, and 3 together to fight like a world champion!

Mike Tyson's Punch Out is a trademark of Nintendo of America Inc.

Millipede™ Game

Ever been annoyed that you can only roam around the bottom of the screen? Well, PEDE Codes 4 and 5 can fix all that! You can now have half or even the whole of the screen to move around—try it . . .it makes the game very different!

PEDE CODE	KEY IN . . .	EFFECT . . .
1	SUKGETVI	Both players have infinite lives

2	PAVKSPGA	Player 1 starts with 1 life
3	ZAVKSPGE	Player 1 starts with 10 lives
4	ASESIIEZ	Increase territory to half screen
5	AXESIIEZ	Increase territory to full screen
6	NKESIIEZ	Shrink territory!
7	ZEUSXYTE	Player's bullets move faster
8	LEUSXYTA	Player's bullets move slower

Remember that you can pick'n'mix your codes! You can enter up to THREE separate codes at one time.

Millipede is a trademark of Atari Corporation. Used by HAL America, Inc., under license.

Mission: Impossible™ Game

MISS Codes 6 and 8 give your agents plenty of extra Type B weapons. And MISS Code 2 gives them some extra energy. To make their disguise last a few seconds longer, use MISS Code 10. For some protection from attacks, try MISS Code 3.

MISS CODE	KEY IN . . .	EFFECT . . .
1	TEOUNKGA	Start with less energy
2	AOOUNKGA	Start with more energy
3	SXUETVOU	Take less damage
4	ZENETTPA	Take more damage
5	ZEULXGIA	2 Type B weapons for Nicholas™
6	PEULXGIE	9 Type B weapons for Nicholas
7	IEXUXKZA	5 Type B weapons for Max™ and Grant™
8	YEXUXKZE	15 Type B weapons for Max and Grant
9	AAUPIZPA	Infinite Type B weapons for all
10	VKOAVOSX + GAEOPLPA	Longer disguise time

Remember that you can pick'n'mix your codes. You can enter up to THREE separate codes at one time.

Mission: Impossible, Nicholas, Max and Grant are trademarks of Paramount Pictures. Used by Ultra Software Corporation under license.

Monopoly™ Game

All these codes for Monopoly™ will alter the amount of money you either collect or pay out. They work for all players. MONO Code 1 gives you an extra $100 each time you pass 'Go'. MONO Code 3 works like a "Get Out of Jail Free™" card. If you hate getting clobbered on the Luxury Tax™, why not bring the cost down a little with MONO Code 5? Have fun, all you entrepreneurs out there!

MONO CODE	KEY IN . . .	EFFECT . . .
1	YLSSOLPU	Collect $300 as you pass Go
2	IPSSOLPU	Collect $100 as you pass Go

Some codes may cause undesired effects (which are not permanent). If this occurs,

3	AAVZKAYP	Pay $0 to get out of jail
4	IPVZKAYO	Pay $100 to get out of jail
5	LOOAVKZP	Pay $30 for Luxury Tax
6	IOOAVKZO	Pay $100 for Luxury Tax
7	PUOAVKZP	Pay $200 for Luxury Tax
8	AESAVGPL	Pay $0 for income tax
9	LOSAVGPL	Pay $30 for income tax
10	IOSAVGPU	Pay $100 for income tax
11	YUSAVGPU	Pay $300 for income tax
12	YLOSLKLK	$300 to buy Boardwalk™
13	LIOSLKLG	$600 to buy Boardwalk
14	PLOIZGIG	$200 to buy Park Place™
15	LGOIZGIK	$400 to buy Park Place
16	LIOIZGIG	$600 to buy Park Place
17	IPOSZGPU	Houses on Park Place cost $100
18	YLOSZGPU	Houses on Park Place cost $300
19	IPXILGPU	Houses on Boardwalk cost $100
20	YLXILGPU	Houses on Boardwalk cost $300
21	YAOAILLA	Go Back 7 spaces instead of 3 on Chance™

Monopoly, Get Out of Jail Free, Luxury Tax, Boardwalk, Park Place and Chance are trademarks of Parker Brothers.

Monster Party™ Game

We have a fistful of level warps for anybody who wants to explore the game, and we also have two codes (PART Codes 3 and 4) which when used together make sure that nothing can hurt you! At the start of the game our hero only has a small amount of energy. If you want more, then use PART Code 1 or 2—they should do the trick!

PART CODE	KEY IN . . .	EFFECT . . .
1	APUPZSGE + AOKPTKGE	Start with boosted energy
2	GZUPZSGE + GXKPTKGE	Start with super-boosted energy
3	SXXAYYVG	Take no damage, except from Guardians™
4	VVXAIYVG	Take no damage from Guardians
5	PAKOZIAA	Start on level 2
6	ZAKOZIAA	Start on level 3
7	LAKOZIAA	Start on level 4
8	GAKOZIAA	Start on level 5
9	IAKOZIAA	Start on level 6
10	TAKOZIAA	Start on level 7

Remember that you can pick'n'mix your codes! You can enter up to THREE separate codes at one time, or one double code (like PART Code 2) and one other code (like PART Code 8).

Monster Party and Guardians are trademarks of Bandai America Inc.

Ms. Pac-Man™ Game

Check out these codes for an excellent Ms. Pac Man! MS Code 7 makes your turbo even faster
—it's great fun! If you'd really like a couple fewer ghosts to contend with, use MS Codes 8 and 9.

MS CODE	KEY IN . . .	EFFECT . . .	
1	AEUAYTZA	1 life for players 1 and 2	
2	IEUAYTZA	6 lives for players 1 and 2	
3	AEUAYTZE	9 lives for players 1 and 2	
4	KEUEZVSE	1 life for player 2 in 2-player cooperative and competitive games	
5	SXNETZVG	Infinite lives for players 1 and 2 in alternating type games	
6	SZEALUVK	Infinite lives for player 2 only, in other type games	
7	XVONINZK	Super fast turbo speed!	
8	AAUEZTZA	Pinky™ out of game	
9	AASEZTZA	Sue™ out of game	

Why not use MS Codes 7, 8 and 9 together for a much easier game?
Ms. Pac-Man, Pinky and Sue are trademarks of Namco, Ltd. Used by Tengen, Inc. under license.

M.U.L.E.™ Game

Players of this fantasy adventure should be excited to see the codes we have for M.U.L.E.™ Some
make it harder to survive and some will help. MULE Codes 2 and 4 give you extra money to
bargain with, and MULE Codes 6 and 8 give you extra time to make your profits!

MULE CODE	KEY IN . . .	EFFECT . . .
1	EPOEPNAI + PAOETYZA	Humanoids start with $400
2	AZOEPNAI + LAOETYZA	Humanoids start with $800
3	GPUAAYAG + IAUAIYTA	Flappers start with $1300
4	EIUAAYAG + YAUAIYTA	Flappers start with $2000
5	GEKALTTA	4 'months' for beginner game
6	PEKALTTE	9 'months' for beginner game
7	TEXAIVGA	6 'months' for standard game
8	GOXAIVGA	20 'months' for standard game

Remember that you can pick'n'mix your codes.
M.U.L.E. is a trademark of Mindscape, Inc.

M.U.S.C.L.E.™ Game

Check out MUSC Codes 1 thru 3 to alter bout lengths. MUSC Code 6 will give your team players
invincibility, or you could try MUSC Codes 4 and 5 to give your opponents the advantage and
make the game harder.

MUSC CODE	KEY IN . . .	EFFECT . . .
1	ZESELPLA	Set bout length timer to 20
2	TESELPLA	Set bout length timer to 60
3	PESELPLE	Set bout length timer to 90

Some codes may cause undesired effects (which are not permanent). If this occurs,

4	ZEUOUPPA	Computer controlled players jump faster
5	ZASXAAPA	Computer controlled players speed up
6	OZUEPZSX + LTUEZXYG	Invincibility player 1 team

Remember you can pick'n'mix codes. Enter up to THREE separate codes at one time or one double code (like MUSC Code 6) and one single code (like MUSC Code 3).
M.U.S.C.L.E. is a trademark of Mattel, Inc.

Mystery Quest™ Game

You normally start Mystery Quest™ with no items in your possession. Now, with the help of the Game Genie™, you can start the game with the key and the SOS raft. Just use MYST Code 6. You can also make sure that you never lose these things—use MYST Codes 7 and 8.

MYST CODE	KEY IN . . .	EFFECT . . .	
1	GXNPYAVG	Invincibility	
2	AEXOGEEY	Immune to monster attacks	
3	AEUOAENY	Immune to shallow water	
4	ATSEUYAG	Start with more energy	
5	AZSEUYAG	Start with less energy	
6	PEUOKPAA	Start with raft and key	
7	GXVOOYSA	Never lose key	
8	PENOPTAA	Never lose raft	

Remember that you can pick'n'mix your codes! You can enter up to THREE separate codes at one time.
Mystery Quest is a trademark of Kabushiki Kaisha Carry Lab. Used by Taxan USA Corp. under license.
Game Genie is a trademark of Lewis Galoob Toys, Inc.

Narc™ Game

These Narc™ codes let YOU choose how many lives, missiles and bullets you want in a perfect game! Some make playing a lot easier, like NARC Codes 4, 8 and 10, while some make it extremely hard, like NARC Codes 1 and 6. Take your pick.

NARC CODE	KEY IN . . .	EFFECT . . .	
1	AAUAZPZA	1 life	
2	IAUAZPZA	6 lives	
3	AAUAZPZE	9 lives	
4	SUKVTLVI	Infinite lives	
5	PUVAGAIU	More missiles	
6	PEUZPZIA	1 missile picked up	
7	PEUZPZIE	9 missile picked up	
8	AEEILGPA	Infinite missiles	
9	GASPTLZA	More bullets picked up	
10	AAOSUPPA	Infinite bullets	

Narc is a trademark of Williams Electronic Games, Inc. Used by Acclaim Entertainment, Inc. under license.

refer to pages 10 and 11 for instructions. If you still have problems, call 1-513-868-8835.

A Nightmare on Elm Street™ Game

Are you frightened of Freddy™? Well, maybe some of these codes can help you. ELM Code 1 gives you infinite lives, ELM Codes 5 and 6 slow down the sleep meter. And ELM Code 8 gives you the power to super jump, right over the heads of those dreaded dream monsters!

ELM CODE	KEY IN . . .	EFFECT . . .	
1	SUELSUVS	Infinite lives	
2	PAUVEZLA	1 continue	
3	TAUVEZLA	6 continues	
4	PAUVEZLE	9 continues	
5	AESSLAEA	Don't lose 'zzz' when hit	
6	AAXOLAPA	Don't lose 'zzz' when standing still	
7	ZAXOLAPA	Lose 'zzz' quicker	
8	IEULIGLA	Mega-jumping teenagers	

Remember that you can pick'n'mix your codes. You can enter up to THREE separate codes at one time.

A Nightmare On Elm Street and Freddy are trademarks of The Fourth New Line-Heron Venture. Used by LJN Toys, Ltd. under license.

Ninja Crusaders™ Game

For this mega-tough ninja game we have some awesome codes to help you out! NINJA Codes 2 thru 4 give you extra lives. NINJA Code 5 gives you super speed and NINJA Code 6 gives you mega-jump. Ninja Codes 7 thru 14 are all-level warps. If you're going to warp to one of the later levels, be sure to take some extra lives and maybe a little jumping power with you—you may need them!

NINJA CODE	KEY IN . . .	EFFECT . . .	
1	PEOZEALA	1 life	
2	TEOZEALA	6 lives	
3	PEOZEALE	9 lives	
4	SLKKAOVS	Infinite lives	
5	SYXESUVN + ZAXEULPA	Super speed Ninjas	
6	IZNXNTZP	Mega-jumping Ninjas	
7	PAEPTGAA	Start on stage 1-2	
8	ZAEPTGAA	Start on stage 2-1	
9	LAEPTGAA	Start on stage 2-2	
10	GAEPTGAA	Start on stage 3-1	
11	IAEPTGAA	Start on stage 3-2	
12	TAEPTGAA	Start on stage 4-1	
13	YAEPTGAA	Start on stage 4-2	
14	AAEPTGAE	Start on stage 5-1	

Ninja Crusaders is a trademark of American Sammy Corp.

    Some codes may cause undesired effects (which are not permanent). If this occurs,

Ninja Gaiden™ Game

For Ninja Gaiden™ we have Game Genie™ codes which stop you from losing spiritual strength when you use various weapons. You can also increase the power of the strength restorers that can be found during the game—just use NINJ Code 8!

NINJ CODE	KEY IN ...	EFFECT ...	
1	SZETPGVG	Infinite lives	
2	AAUVLIZE	Start with 9 lives	
3	IAUVLIZA	Start with 6 lives	
4	AAUVLIZA	Start with 1 life	
5	AEXVVYIA	Use windmill throwing-star without losing spiritual strength	
6	AAETUYIA	Use fire-wheel without losing spiritual strength	
7	AAVTNYLA	Use shuriken without losing spiritual strength	
8	APEIKGTA	Maximum strength regained from restorer	

Remember that you can pick'n'mix your codes! You can enter up to THREE separate codes at one time.

Ninja Gaiden is a trademark of Tecmo, Inc.
Game Genie is a trademark of Lewis Galoob Toys, Inc.

Ninja Gaiden II™ Game

Ryu™ is back in yet another amazing adventure! With the help of Game Genie™, his ninja power can be improved using GAID Codes 12, 13, and 14. Also, check out GAID Codes 15 and 16 to give Ryu turbo-running power! There's loads more codes to help your quest for fun, so give them all a try.

GAID CODE	KEY IN ...	EFFECT ...	
1	AEKGVTZA	Start with 1 life	
2	IEKGVTZA + SEKKKTSP	Start with 6 lives	
3	AEKGVTZE + SEKKKTSP	Start with 9 lives	
4	SXXGXAVG	Infinite lives	
5	SZNGKGSA	Almost invincible!	
6	LEUOSATA	Half-energy from medicine	
7	GEUOSATE	Double energy from medicine	
8	IAUONEZA + IAKOOEZA	Half-energy from Blue Ninja power	
9	GPUONEZA + GPKOOEZA	Double energy from Blue Ninja power	
10	GOEPOEZA + ZEOOEAPA	Double maximum Ninja power from scroll	

11	SXVKLTVG	Stop timer
12	SVOPXXSN + SVOOKXSN + SVXOXXSN	All powers use up only 5 points
13	XXEOSZVZ + LOEOVXIY + PUOOSXLK	Infinite Ninja power
14	GXKKUIVA	Never lose Ninja power item
15	ZEXGYAPA + SNEKYEVN	Fast running Ryu
16	LEXGYAPA + KNEKYEVN	Mega-fast running Ryu

Pick'n'mix your codes, and try GAID Codes 5 and 15 for a Mega-Ninja!

Ninja Gaiden II and Ryu are trademarks of Tecmo, Inc.
Game Genie is a trademark of Lewis Galoob Toys, Inc.

Ninja Kid™ Game

There's plenty of codes here for Game Genie™ fans. Try out KID Codes 1 thru 3 for life adjustment. You can have an infinite supply of weapons with KID Codes 4 thru 7. If you don't want infinite weapons, then you can always use KID Codes 8 thru 14 to get a varied number of different weapons—just take your pick!

KID CODE	KEY IN . . .	EFFECT . . .
1	AAVEZAZA	Start with 1 life
2	IAVEZAZA	Start with 6 lives
3	AAVEZAZE	Start with 9 lives
4	SZOZUPVG	Infinite Feathers
5	SZXXITVG	Infinite Stars
6	SXNOGGVG	Infinite Boomerangs
7	SXUZZYVG	Infinite Fireflames
8	PAXSXALA	Only 1 Feather picked up
9	TAXSXALA	6 Feathers picked up
10	ZAXSUAGO	Only 10 Stars picked up
11	AZXSUAGO	40 Stars picked up
12	ZAXSKAGA	Only 1 Boomerang picked up
13	ZAXSSAGO	Only 10 Fireflames picked up
14	AZXSSAGO	40 Fireflames picked up
15	YAEILNYA	Less Invincibility time
16	AZEILNYE	More Invincibility time

Ninja Kid is a trademark of Bandai America, Inc.
Game Genie is a trademark of Lewis Galoob Toys, Inc.

North & South™ Game

Now you can change the tactics of this game. You can restrict the use of cannons for both sides with NORTH Code 1, or else have an infinite amount of daggers in the fortress with NORTH Code 6. NORTH Codes 7 and 9 give the player defending his fortress or train only two men to keep the enemy at bay.

Some codes may cause undesired effects (which are not permanent). If this occurs,

NORTH CODE	KEY IN...	EFFECT...	
1	IEUATOPA	Cannon has 5 shots	
2	YEUATOPE	Cannon has 15 shots	
3	SZXPYUVS	Cannon has infinite shots	
4	GXXATOSO	No cannons allowed!	
5	ZAUAGPGA	Only 2 daggers in the fortress	
6	GXXPLKVS	Infinite daggers in the fortress	
7	ZAUETOZA	2 men in the fortress	
8	IAUETOZA	5 men in the fortress	
9	ZASAGOZA	2 men on the train	
10	IASAGOZA	5 men on the train	

Remember that you can pick'n'mix your codes. You can enter up to THREE separate codes at one time.
North & South is a trademark of Infogrames.

Operation Wolf™ Game

As well as some level warps (OP Codes 3 thru 7), we have codes to make sure that you don't take any damage from enemy fire (OP Code 2), and to give you infinite ammunition (OP Codes 8 and 9). An interesting code for the player who is already fairly accomplished is OP Code 13, which makes sure that you return to the peak of health at the end of each level.

OP CODE	KEY IN ...	EFFECT ...	
1	IEVUNSPA	Infinite continues	
2	AESSLZTL	Never die	
3	PESZIGAA	Start on mission 2	
4	ZESZIGAA	Start on mission 3	
5	LESZIGAA	Start on mission 4	
6	GESZIGAA	Start on mission 5	
7	IESZIGAA	Start on mission 6	
8	AAVSIIPA	Infinite magazines	
9	AAEIATPA	Infinite grenades	
10	PEVKVYYE + PAVSIIIE	Increase magazines	
11	PENGXYIE + PAVSIILE	Increase grenades	
12	GANIYIZA	Double bullets in each magazine	
13	NNESZALE	Heal completely between levels	
14	GANULZZA	Grenades inflict double damage	
15	ZAELGPIE	Super power drinks	

Remember that you can pick'n'mix your codes! You can enter up to THREE separate codes at one time, or one double-code (like OP Code 11) and one single code (like OP Code 13).
Operation Wolf is a trademark of Taito America Corporation.

P.O.W.™ Game

POW Codes 1 thru 4 give you a choice of lives to suit your ability. POW Code 5 starts you off with less energy. And POW Code 6 gives you protection against attacks from behind. Once you have found the machine gun, POW Code 8 gives you infinite bullets! And POW Code 7 lets you keep your weapons after losing a life.

POW CODE	KEY IN ...	EFFECT ...
1	AEUEIZZA	1 life
2	IEUEIZZA	6 lives
3	AEUEIZZE	9 lives
4	AENSLPPA	Infinite lives
5	APKGPLAZ + APESYZAZ	Play with less energy
6	STOLOUON	Take less damage when hit from behind
7	GZUUNUSE + GZSLOSSE	Keep weapons
8	AAVGOTPA	Infinite bullets

P.O.W. is a trademark of SNK Corp. of America.

Pac Man™ Game

Everyone in the known universe must have learned to play this game well by now. To make the game more difficult, PAC Code 4 makes the effect of the power pills last for a shorter time, while PAC Codes 6 and 7 make some of the ghosts immune to the effects of the power pills. Wocka wocka wocka, woooo woooo woooo . . .

PAC CODE	KEY IN ...	EFFECT ...
1	SZEKKIVG	Both players have infinite lives
2	VTGKVZ	1 life for player 2
3	AYVITOGL	Power pills last longer
4	AZVITOGL	Power pills don't last as long
5	ATXTZASZ	Power pills don't work
6	IAXVYEYE	Only 3 ghosts are edible
7	PAXVYEYE	Only 2 ghosts are edible

Remember that you can pick'n'mix your codes! You can enter up to THREE separate codes at one time.
Pac Man is a trademark of Atari Games Corp. Used by Namco, Ltd., under license.

Paper Boy™ Game

Paper Boy™ should be a breeze if you use BOY Codes 1 and 4 to give you infinite lives and infinite papers. You can also make sure that you pick up 20 papers in every bundle by using BOY Code 6.

Some codes may cause undesired effects (which are not permanent). If this occurs,

BOY
CODE   KEY IN . . .   EFFECT . . .

1   SXSEVZVG   Infinite lives

2   PAUOEIGA   Start with 1 life
3   TAUOEIGA   Start with 6 lives

4   OZNOKAVK   Infinite papers

5   GOXAUOZA   Start with 20 papers

6   GPUONUZA   Gain 20 papers on pick-up

Remember, you can program your own codes! BOY Codes 2 and 3 might make good codes to try your programming luck on!
Paper Boy is a trademark of Tengen.

Phantom Fighter™ Game

To help Kenchi™ fight the phantoms, check out these codes! With PHAN Codes 1 thru 4 you can choose to start the game with your favorite weapon. To build your ninja skills, use PHAN Code 8 to give you more stamina for fighting and help you through the game.

PHAN
CODE   KEY IN . . .   EFFECT . . .

1   VTVKEGSA + KAVKOGNA   Start with Sword
2   VTVKEGSA + SAVKOGNA   Start with Bell
3   VTVKEGSA + UAVKOGNA   Start with Tonten
4   VTVKEGSA + XAVKOGNA   Start with Talisman
5   LASKNGAA + VAVKOGNA   Start with 3 Scrolls
6   TASKNGAA + VAVKOGNA   Start with 6 Scrolls

7   SXSZLUSE   Infinite energy

8   OVSZPLSV + PESZZLAA   Take less damage when attacked

Remember that you can pick'n'mix your codes.
Phantom Fighter and Kenchi are trademarks of Fujisankei Communications International, Inc.

Pin-Bot™ Game

BOT Code 1 is handy if you're playing with friends—it makes each game shorter so your turn comes around quicker! If you want to see the whole game through, use BOT Code 4 for infinite balls.

BOT
CODE   KEY IN . . .   EFFECT . . .

1   PANTGZLA   Start with only 1 ball
2   TANTGZLA   Start with 6 balls
3   PANTGZLE   Start with 9 balls

4   OZVVYZVV   Infinite balls

Pin-Bot is a trademark of Williams Electronic Games, Inc.

Pinball Game

Hey, pinball wizards, get your fingers on those flippers, 'cause here's some codes to really get you rolling! Make playing harder or easier—the choice is yours.

PIN CODE	KEY IN . . .	EFFECT . . .	
1	PASGPALA	Start game with 1 ball	
2	TASGPALA	Start game with 6 balls	
3	PASGPALE	Start game with 9 balls	
4	SUXKLEVS	Infinite balls in 'B' game	

Pipe Dream™ Game

PIPE Codes 1 thru 4 change the number of wrenches you start with, which in Pipe Dream™ count as your lives! If you find using the one-way pipes difficult, you can use PIPE Codes 6 and 7 so they won't appear until the later levels. For loads of tunnels, check out PIPE Code 8, and for extra pumps see PIPE Codes 9 and 10.

PIPE CODE	KEY IN . . .	EFFECT . . .	
1	PAOALPLA	Start with 1 wrench	
2	TAOALPLA	Start with 6 wrenches	
3	PAOALPLE	Start with 9 wrenches	
4	SZKTPUVK	Infinite wrenches	
5	AAOGZZIA	One-way pipes from level 1	
6	IAOGAZLA	One-way pipes from level 5	
7	ZAOKPZLE	One-way pipes from level 10	
8	KEUAUVSE	Tunnels galore	
9	GPKIEGZP + ZPKINGGP	Pumps before reservoirs	
10	GPKIEGZP	Pumps instead of reservoirs	

Remember that you can pick'n'mix your codes.

Pipe Dream is a trademark of Lucasarts Entertainment Company. Used by Bullet-Proof Software under license.

Platoon™ Game

We've split the codes for Platoon™ into groups for each level of the game. As usual, just look down the list, pick out a couple of tasty codes, and give 'em a try!

PLAT CODE	KEY IN . . .	EFFECT . . .	
STAGE 1			
1	SXKOZPVG	Infinite grenades	
2	SZSPYAVG	Start with double capacity magazine	
3	AEKESYGE	Double hits	
4	SXKAUYVT	Don't take damage	
STAGE 2			
5	GAKEAPIA	Start on stage 2	

Some codes may cause undesired effects (which are not permanent). If this occurs,

| 6 | SZVAXTVT | Don't take damage | |

STAGE 3

| 7 | LAEGGATA | Start on stage 3 | |

STAGE 4

8	SXKEUZVG	Freeze timer	
9	IEVEOPLA	Play with more time	
10	PAKOIPIE	Double hits	
11	ZAKOIPIA	Halve hits	
12	GEXEUPTE	Start with double ammo	

Platoon is a trademark of Hemdale Film Corporation. Used by Sun Corporation of America under license

Popeye™ Game

POP Codes 2 through 4 make Popeye™ harder or easier, or you can explore the game with POP Code 1.

PRED CODE	KEY IN . . .	EFFECT . . .	
1	GSGKXG	Infinite lives for Popeye	
2	PAPKNA	1 life for Popeye	
3	TAPKNA	6 lives for Popeye	
4	PAPKNE	9 lives for Popeye	

Popeye is a trademark of King Features Syndicate, Inc. Used by Nintendo of America, Inc. under license.

Predator™ Game

When playing Predator™ you can use PRED Code 7 to ensure that you don't die if you fall down a hole. However, if you get stuck you must self-destruct! PRED Code 4 makes sure that you start each life/level with a nice shiny laser rifle—the film would have been over in 20 minutes if Arnie had it as easy as you do with the Game Genie™!

PRED CODE	KEY IN . . .	EFFECT . . .	
1	SZNGGXVK	Infinite lives in jungle mode	
2	SXXGZOVK	Infinite lives in big mode	
3	AAVKGPGE	Start with double lives	
4	LASEOELA + XLSEUEVX	Start each life with laser rifle	
5	AVUGVGSA	Infinite life points in jungle mode	
6	AEOETOPE	Mega-jumps in jungle mode	
7	NTEENEGE + ATOAEEOZ	Don't die if you fall down holes	

Remember that you can pick'n'mix your codes! You can enter up to THREE separate codes at one time, or one double-code (like PRED Code 4) and one single code (like PRED Code 3).

Predator is a trademark of Twentieth Century Fox. Used by Activision under license.
Game Genie is a trademark of Lewis Galoob Toys, Inc.

refer to pages 10 and 11 for instructions. If you still have problems, call 1-513-868-8835.

109

The Punisher™ Game

PUN Codes 1 and 2 give you a choice of lives. PUN Codes 3 and 4 keep you from losing lives in conflicts with the enemy. For unlimited ammo supplies, check out PUN Codes 5 and 6, and for some extra energy see PUN Code 11.

PUN CODES	KEY IN . . .	EFFECT . . .	
1	PEOTYTIA	1 life	
2	ZEOTYTIE	10 lives	
3	XVOVGXXK	Never lose a life against normal enemy	
4	XVOEXOXK	Never lose a life against end of level enemy	
5	XTSVSNXK	Infinite grenades	
6	AESYAPPA	Infinite bullets and rockets	
7	GEUUYIZA	Faster Punisher™	
8	PEUYNLAA	Pick up 150 machine pistol bullets	
9	PEUNXLAA	Pick up 150 assault rifle bullets	
10	AAEUUPAO	Less energy picked up	
11	APEUUPAO	More energy picked up	

Remember that you can pick'n'mix your codes. You can enter up to THREE separate codes at one time.
The Punisher is a trademark of Marvel Entertainment Group, Inc. Used by LJN Toys, Ltd. under license.

Puss 'n Boots—Pero's Great Adventure™ Game

We have all the regular life, energy and level-warp codes for you to try in this cat-astrophic adventure! Our star code for this game is BOOT Code 11 for autofire and autojump!

BOOT CODE	KEY IN . . .	EFFECT . . .	
1	PEOGZALA	Start with 1 life	
2	TEOGZALA	Start with 6 lives	
3	PEOGZALE	Start with 9 lives	
4	SZOKZZVG	Infinite lives	
5	GOSTNUAU	Start with less energy	
6	SZNGOISA	Infinite energy	
7	GAEGAIAA	Start on stage 1	
8	PAEGAIAE	Start on stage 2	
9	TAEGAIAE	Start on stage 3	
10	AAXGNUPA	Mega-jump	
11	AAOVNENY	Autofire and Autojump	

Remember that you can pick'n'mix codes. You can enter up to THREE separate codes at one time.
Puss 'n Boots—Pero's Great Adventure is a trademark of Toei Animation. Used by Electro Brain Corp. under license.

Some codes may cause undesired effects (which are not permanent). If this occurs,

Q*Bert™ Game

There are a brace of Game Genie™ codes to change the playability of this colorful game. As well as being able to choose how many lives you have (BERT Codes 1 thru 3), you can also warp to levels using BERT Codes 4 thru 6.

BERT CODE	KEY IN...	EFFECT...	
1	SXSZGPVG	Infinite lives	
2	PEUOOGIA + PAXZLLIA	Start with 1 life	
3	ZAXZLLIE + ZEUOOGIE	Start with 10 lives	
4	AESPVGAE	Start on level 3	
5	GOSPVGAA	Start on level 6	
6	AXSPVGAA	Start on level 9	

Remember that you can pick'n'mix your codes! You can enter up to THREE separate codes at one time, or one double-code (like BERT Code 3) and one single code (like BERT Code 6).

Q*BERT is a trademark of JVW Electronics, Inc. Used by Konami Inc. under license.
Game Genie is a trademark of Lewis Galoob Toys, Inc.

Qix™ Game

Check out some of the later levels with QIX™ Codes 3 thru 8. Try starting a friend on a higher level and see if you can catch up! Also, make the game harder with QIX Codes 1 and 2.

QIX CODE	KEY IN...	EFFECT...	
1	PEEAPZGA	1 life for player 1	
2	PEEEAZGA	1 life for player 2	
3	IANAZZPA	Start on Level 5, player 1 game	
4	ZANAZZPE	Start on Level 10, player 1 game	
5	GPNAZZPA	Start on Level 20, player 1 game	
6	IEEEGZPA	Start on Level 5, player 2 game	
7	ZEEEGZPE	Start on Level 10, player 2 game	
8	GOEEGZPA	Start on Level 20, player 2 game	

Remember that you can pick'n'mix your codes. You can enter up to THREE separate codes at one time.

Qix is a trademark of Taito America Corporation.

Rad Racer™ Game

Turn the key and rev that engine—the race is on! If you're an ace racer, why not try RAD Code 1 to make things a bit tougher. Bolt on a turbo and make your car accelerate faster with RAD Codes 8, 9, or 10. Try each one to see which suits your driving style.

RAD CODE	KEY IN...	EFFECT...	
1	GZXIUVIZ	Less time to finish each stage	
2	GLXIUVIX	More time to finish each stage	

3	PAXKPAAA + GXKGKTSA	Start at stage 2
4	ZAXKPAAA + GXKGKTSA	Start at stage 3
5	LAXKPAAA + GXKGKTSA	Start at stage 4
6	GAXKPAAA + GXKGKTSA	Start at stage 5
7	IAXKPAAA + GXKGKTSA	Start at stage 6
8	ALXGAIAA	Turbo acceleration
9	YYUKGIAU	Super Turbo acceleration
10	PEEGPIAA	Ultra Turbo acceleration

Pick'n'mix your favorite codes to help you through the race!
Rad Racer is a trademark of Square Soft, Inc.

Raid on Bungeling Bay™ Game

To make your raid a bit easier, we have Game Genie™ codes to make sure that your helicopter is invincible (RAID Code 4) and to give you an infinite supply of bombs (RAID Code 3). You can also warp to later levels using RAID Codes 5 thru 7.

RAID CODE	KEY IN . . .	EFFECT . . .
1	PENGZYIE	Start with 9 lives
2	PENGZYIA	Start with 1 life
3	SXSIASVK	Infinite bombs
4	SXVVPIAX	Take no damage from ANYTHING
5	LEVKTYPA	Start on round 3
6	TEVKTYPA	Start on round 6
7	PEVKTYPE	Start on round 9
8	AZOIIEGX	You can only carry 5 bombs

Remember that you can pick'n'mix your codes! You can enter up to THREE separate codes at one time. You might try RAID Code 3 and RAID Code 4 together to explore the whole game.
Raid on Bungeling Bay is a trademark of Broderbund Software, Inc.
Game Genie is a trademark of Lewis Galoob Toys, Inc.

Rally Bike™ Game

Here's a whole bunch of codes for changing the number of lives the players start with. You can use them to get further in the game, or to give an extra edge to one player. Also, check out RAL Code 7, which makes sure that you won't ever have to stop for gas again!

RAL CODE	KEY IN . . .	EFFECT . . .
1	PAUIKTIA	Start with 1 life in 1-player game
2	ZAUIKTIE	Start with 10 lives in 1-player game
3	PAUIKITA + ZAXSTGTA	Start with 1 life in 2-player game, both players
4	ZAUIKTIE + LAXSTGIE	Start with 10 lives in 2-player game, both players
5	SZEITKVV	Infinite lives in 1 player game
6	SZOSIKVN	Infinite lives in 2 player game, both players

Some codes may cause undesired effects (which are not permanent). If this occurs,

| 7 | SIUKLUVV | Infinite gas |

Remember that you can pick'n'mix your codes. RAL Codes 5 and 7 together make for an easier game.

Rally Bike is a trademark of Romstar, Incorporated.

Rambo™ Game

Rambo™ is another game for which we have the highly useful 'keep weapons after death' Game Genie™ code—BO Code 1 will do the trick. If you'd like to start the game with some slightly heavier weaponry, then check out BO Codes 6 thru 9, or if you want to pick up double quantities of everything then use BO Code 10.

BO CODE	KEY IN . . .	EFFECT . . .	
1	SXOVXKVS	Never lose weapons	
2	GZXVXUVS	Never lose medicine bottles	
3	ZEEEITIE	Double medicine bottles	
4	GOEAPVZA	Double throwing knives	
5	ZEEEITIA	Start with 2 medicine bottles	
6	ZPNEITPP + ZOEALTPP	Start with bow and arrows	
7	LPNEITPP + LOEALTPP	Start with exploding arrows	
8	GPNEITPP + GOEALTPP	Start with machine gun	
9	IPNEITPP + IOEALTPP	Start with hand grenades	
10	GOXTZXZA	Gain double items on pick-up	

Remember that you can pick'n'mix your codes! You can enter up to THREE separate codes at one time, or one double-code (like BO Code 8) and one single code (like BO Code 1).

Rambo is a trademark of Carolco. Used by Acclaim Entertainment, Inc., under license.
Game Genie is a trademark of Lewis Galoob Toys, Inc.

Rampage™ Game

Plenty of codes here to give you a helping hand in this monster game! Also, a few codes to make playing harder for one or both players. Be sure to check out RAM Code 12 for a harder game—it only allows half the normal energy boost from food.

RAM CODE	KEY IN . . .	EFFECT . . .
1	NYSGLUYN	More energy for player 1
2	NYVKTUYN	More energy for player 2
3	YLSGLUYN	Less energy for player 1
4	YLVKTUYN	Less energy for player 2
5	NNNGKNYN	More energy for players 1 and 2 after continue
6	YUNGKNYN	Less energy for players 1 and 2 after continue

refer to pages 10 and 11 for instructions. If you still have problems, call 1-513-868-8835.

113

7	AAOUOPPA + AASLSPPA	No harm from water
8	AEXLPGAP	No harm from falling
9	GXXLALOP	No harm from attacks or bad food
10	AXXLPGAP	More damage done from falling
11	GEULLLIA	Double energy from food
12	AEULLLIA + ZKULTUZE	Half energy from food

Remember that you can pick'n'mix codes. Enter up to THREE separate codes at one time or one single code (like RAM Code 5) and one double code (like RAM Code 7).

Rampage is a trademark of Bally Midway Manufacturing Co. used by Data East USA, Inc. under license.

RC Pro Am™ Game

A few more continues will always come in handy in this game—use PRO Codes 1 thru 4 to select the number of continues that you'd like. (Just one continue is always useful if you have a bunch of friends around!) You can also customize your car—for example, just one turbo pick-up could see your car with the full turbo add-on! And check out Code 11—it makes the computer cars go crazy . . . after half a lap or so . . . wait for it!

PRO CODE	KEY IN . . .	EFFECT . . .
1	AAEIPPPA	Infinite continues
2	AEXEPPZA	No continues
3	IEXEPPZA	5 continues
4	AEXEPPZE	8 continues
5	GEUGAPPA	Max turbo on first pick-up
6	GEKKGPPA	Max tires on first pick-up
7	GAVGIPPA	Max speed on first pick-up
8	ZEUGAPPA	Double turbo on first pick-up
9	ZEKKGPPA	Double tires on first pick-up
10	ZAVGIPPA	Double speed on first pick-up
11	SXVLGZAK	Computer cars go crazy!

Remember that you can pick'n'mix your codes! You can enter up to THREE separate codes at one time.

RC Pro Am is a trademark of Nintendo of America Inc.

Renegade™ Game

There's a good lot of Game Genie™ codes for this popular "beat 'em up" game. We've got codes to warp thru missions, codes to vary lives, a code to give an energy boost, codes that fool around with the timer, and, of course, the obligatory infinite lives code . . . check 'em out!
NOTE: Code 5 does provide an energy boost. The display maxes out at 16 bars, but you get more—check out how you can take some damage before it starts to count down.

PRO CODE	KEY IN . . .	EFFECT . . .
1	SXUIOTVG	Infinite lives
2	AEOSLYZA	Both players start with 1 life
3	IEOSLYZA	Both players start with 6 lives
4	AEOSLYZE	Both players start with 9 lives

Some codes may cause undesired effects (which are not permanent). If this occurs,

5	AIUOZUAZ	Start with a super energy boost
6	PEXSYYAA	Start on mission 2
7	ZEXSYYAA	Start on mission 3
8	LEXSYYAA	Start on mission 4
9	TOSVOXTU	Timer runs faster
10	EXSVOXTL	Timer runs slower

Remember that you can pick'n'mix your codes! You can enter up to THREE separate codes at one time.

Renegade is a trademark of Taito America Corporation.
Game Genie is a trademark of Lewis Galoob Toys, Inc.

Ring King™ Game

KING Code 1 gives you unlimited power in a one-player game—you can raise all three of your attributes as high as 99 if you wish. There is, however, a catch . . . your computer opponent will be given skills that match yours! KING Code 5 is useful for practicing complicated moves—both players can spar without hurting each other.

KING CODE	KEY IN . . .	EFFECT . . .
1	GZEIPVVK	Unlimited power in 1-player game
2	GXKZXYOP	Don't lose stamina from fighting
3	LEOSLYTA	Cut timer to 30 seconds
4	PEOSLYTE	Boost timer to 90 seconds
5	GXOZOIOP	Players can't hurt each other!

Remember, you can program your own codes! KING Codes 3 and 4 might make good codes to try your programming luck on!

Ring King is a trademark of Data East USA, Inc.

River City Ransom™ Game

Some extra money would come in handy, dontcha think? Well, CITY Codes 3 thru 6 can handle that for you . . . CITY Code 1 is particularly interesting—it gives you a double helping of every status attribute at the beginning of the game. What are you waiting for?—go on and try these codes!

CITY CODE	KEY IN . . .	EFFECT . .
1	TOSNAVYE	Start with double every attribute!
2	LVNYIVYL	Increase stamina to 99
3	AGENAYAZ	Player 1 starts with double money
4	AGOYYYAZ	Player 2 starts with double money
5	PAENIYAA	Player 1 starts with $100 extra
6	PAONGYAA	Player 2 starts with $100 extra

Remember that you can pick'n'mix your codes! You can enter up to THREE separate codes at one time.

River City Ransom is a trademark of Technos Japan Corp.

refer to pages 10 and 11 for instructions. If you still have problems, call 1-513-868-8835.

Road Runner™ Game

Beep beep!!™ Your Road Runner™ can be given the jump on crafty ole' Wile E. Coyote™ with BEEP Code 2, which makes sure that your seed level never goes down . . . the upshot is that you never need to stop to pick any more up! There is also a whole bunch of level warps (BEEP Codes 6 thru 11) for you to play with.

BEEP CODE	KEY IN . . .	EFFECT . . .	
1	SZOVUUVK	Infinite lives	
2	XVUGAOEK + XVXTSUEK	Never lose seed	
3	AAEVTGIA	Start game with 1 life	
4	LAEVTGIE	Start game with 12 lives	
5	PPEVTGIA	Start game with 18 lives	
6	IAOTLGPA	Start at level 5	
7	ZAOTLGPE	Start at level 10	
8	YAOTLGPE	Start at level 15	
9	GPOTLGPA	Start at level 20	
10	PPOTLGPE	Start at level 25	
11	TPOTLGPE	Start at level 30	

Remember that you can pick'n'mix your codes! You can enter up to THREE separate codes at one time, or BEEP Code 2 and one other BEEP Code.

Road Runner, Beep beep!! and Wile E. Coyote are trademarks of Warner Bros. Inc. Used by Tengen under license

Roadblasters™ Game

Lots of codes for this mega-game! Look down the list and you'll see that you can choose what weapons you start the game with, as well as whether or not you have an infinite supply of them. ROAD Codes 1 and 2 help you with extra credits, so that you can get farther into the game.

ROAD CODE	KEY IN . . .	EFFECT . . .	
1	SZEIGEVK	Infinite credits	
2	GAVLUTZA	Double credits	
3	ATNEEISZ	Infinite UZ Cannon	
4	LZOENSTO	Start with UZ Cannon (MUST be used with ROAD Code 3)	
5	PEEAEIIE	Extend lifetime of UZ Cannon	
6	AVSEKSVG	Infinite Nitro Injectors	
7	SAOENSTO + GXKEOIEY	Start with Nitro Injector (MUST be used with ROAD Code 6)	
8	NNSEOIEE	Extend lifetime of Nitro Injector	
9	AKSEOIEA	Reduce lifetime of Nitro Injector	
10	SXVEKSVK	Infinite Cruise missiles	
11	ETOENSTP	Start with Cruise missiles (MUST be used with ROAD Code 10)	

Some codes may cause undesired effects (which are not permanent). If this occurs,

12	SZSEKVVK	Infinite Electro Shield
13	PIOENSTP + VAXAESSE	Start with Electro Shield (MUST be used with ROAD Code 12)

Remember that you can pick'n'mix you codes! You'll find that some ROAD Codes have to be used together; for example, you should use ROAD Codes 6 and 7 at the same time to get permanent Nitro Injection.

Roadblasters is a trademark of Tengen. Used by Mindscape Inc. under license

RoboCop™ Game

Need more time to comply? Try COP Code 1! We all know that RoboCop™ is afraid of nothing—especially when he uses COP Codes 3 and 4 to stop him from taking any damage. However, arguably the best way to protect the innocent is to use COP Code 2 with COP Code 14—it's a real gas!

COP CODE	KEY IN ...	EFFECT ...	
1	SXKXYIVT	Infinite time	
2	SGOTKLIA	Infinite ammunition	
3	SZKVOTSA	Won't take damage from touching enemies	
4	SZVVVYSA	Won't take damage from enemy bullets	
5	PAOYNILE	Triple normal power on power food pick-up	
6	PAXNEILE	Triple normal time on battery pick-up	
7	TPXNEILA	Max time on battery pick-up	
8	TPOYNILA	Full power on power food pick-up	
9	PAESZPAA + SAESLPSP + TTESGPSA	Start on level 2	
10	ZAESZPAA + SAESLPSP + TTESGPSA	Start on level 3	
11	LAESZPAA + SAESLPSP + TTESGPSA	Start on level 4	
12	GAESZPAA + SAESLPSP + TTESGPSA	Start on evel 5	
13	IAESZPAA + SAESLPSP + TTESGPSA	Start on level 6	
14	YAXSAPPE	Use with COP Code 2 to start with machine gun and Cobra gun!	

Remember that you can pick'n'mix your codes! You can use EITHER a level warp OR up to three of the other COP Codes.

RoboCop is a trademark of Orion Pictures Corporation. Used by Data East USA, Inc., under license

refer to pages 10 and 11 for instructions. If you still have problems, call 1-513-868-8835.

117

RoboWarrior™ Game

Among the loads of Game Genie™ codes for RoboWarrior™, there are codes to ensure that you don't take any damage (ROBO Codes 1 and 2) and codes to give you a headstart in the game (ROBO Codes 6 and 7). ROBO Code 5 makes sure that the computer forgets to count down how many super bombs you have when you use them, in effect giving you infinite super bombs!

ROBO CODE	KEY IN . . .	EFFECT . . .
1	GZUNYXTK	Don't take damage from bomb blast
2	GZNNIXTK	Don't take damage from monsters/stops power drain
3	IAVTPSZA	Gain 5 super bombs on pick-up
4	GPVTPSZA	Gain 20 super bombs on pick-up
5	SZKTYPVG	Never use up super bombs
6	IEVKLPAA	Start with 5 of everything!
7	ZEVKLPAE	Start with 10 of everything!
8	IANGAPPA	Set firing range to 5
9	ZANGAPPE	Set firing range to 10
10	IEVGIPPA	Start with Defense Level at 5
11	AEVGIPPE	Start with Defense Level at 8

Remember, you can pick 'n' mix your own codes!

RoboWarrior is a trademark of Jaleco USA Inc.
Game Genie is a trademark of Lewis Galoob Toys, Inc.

Rocket Ranger™ Game

Rocket Ranger™ fans can now adjust the game to suit their needs! Nearly all ROCK Codes will help you in your quest to defeat the evil aliens. ROCK Code 3 will lessen your Lunarium™ in storage, so you'll have to plan your trips carefully!

ROCK CODE	KEY IN . . .	EFFECT . . .
1	ZEOGSYPA	Double amount of Lunarium in storage
2	LEOGSYPA	Triple amount of Lunarium in storage
3	AEOGSYPA + ZUOKNYAA	Half amount of Lunarium in storage
4	LVOKXNGL	Lunarium level in backpack at 99
5	SZSGPUSE	Never lose Lunarium in backpack

Rocket Ranger and Lunarium are trademarks of Cinemaware Corporation.

Some codes may cause undesired effects (which are not permanent). If this occurs,

Roller Ball™ Game

Okay high-rollers, listen up. We've got two most excellent Game Genie™ codes for your use. You can test your skills by using ROLL Code 1 to start with only one ball. Likewise, if you want hours and hours of rolling fun, give ROLL Code 2 a whirl!

ROLL CODE	KEY IN ...	EFFECT ...	
1	PANGIPLA	All players start with only 1 ball	
2	SZKGPXVS	Infinite balls for all players	

Roller Ball is a trademark of Hal America, Inc.
Game Genie is a trademark of Lewis Galoob Toys, Inc.

Rollergames™ Game

Check out the Game Genie™ codes for this game. We've got loads! GAMES Codes 8 thru 10 will allow you to adjust the timer to suit your needs. For the battle against the bad guys, try GAMES Codes 2 thru 4 and give them something to worry about.

GAMES CODE	KEY IN ...	EFFECT ...	
1	SXENAYVG	Infinite lives	
2	PASAZALE	9 special moves	
3	TASAZALA	6 special moves	
4	GXVPAZVG	Infinite special moves	
5	TASATEGA	Start with less energy	
6	APSATEGE	Start with more energy	
7	PAKAAGAE	Mega-jump	
8	GZOENISA	Stop timer	
9	YPOAUSYU	Faster timer	
10	YYOAUSYU	Slower timer	

Remember that you can pick'n'mix your codes. You can enter up to THREE separate codes at one time.

Rollergames is a trademark of World Alliance of Rollersports.
Game Genie is a trademark of Lewis Galoob Toys, Inc.

Rolling Thunder™ Game

Millions (well, quite a lot) of codes you can program for Rolling Thunder™! You can change how many lives you start the game with, how many you have after a continue, how many bullets you pick up at a time, and even stop the timer countdown. Our favorite is ROLL Code 16, which gives you more bullets just as you run out—it's a great one for impressing your pals!

ROLL CODE	KEY IN ...	EFFECT ...	
1	SZNTULVG + SZSTULVG	Infinite lives	
2	PEOVLALA	Start with 1 life	
3	TEOVLALA	Start with 6 lives	
4	PEOVLALE	Start with 9 lives	
5	SZEVYZVG	Stop timer	

---

refer to pages 10 and 11 for instructions. If you still have problems, call 1-513-868-8835.

6	PASPYZLA	Start with 1 life after continue	
7	TASPYZLA	Start with 6 lives after continue	
8	PASPYZLE	Start with 9 lives after continue	
9	AEEVSAZE	Start with increased life meter	
10	EKSTEAGV	200 machine gun bullets on pick-up	
11	SUOZPXVS	300 machine gun bullets on pick-up	
12	GOKVNAZL	Gain fewer bullets on pick-up	
13	LEXTZAAA + LAKTKLAA	Start with loads of ammunition!	
14	EKXVZAZU	Start with 200 bullets	
15	EGKVKLZU	200 bullets on each new life	
16	ZLVITYPA	Self-replenishing bullets!	

Remember, you can program your own codes! ROLL Codes 2 through 4, 6 through 8, 10, 11, 14 and 15 all might make good codes to try your programming luck on!

Rolling Thunder is a trademark of Namco, Ltd. Used by Tengen under license

Rush'N'Attack™ Game

RUSH Code 7 ensures that you never lose POW, in effect making it infinite! There's also a whole load of Game Genie™ codes to change how many lives you have. You can fix the gameplay in either player's favor if you use the codes right.

RUSH CODE	KEY IN . . .	EFFECT . . .	
1	GZOEAYVG	Infinite lives—player 1	
2	GZOEIYVG	Infinite lives—player 2	
3	PAVSTPIA	Start with 1 life—player 1	
4	PANITPIA	Start with 1 life—player 2	
5	ZAVSTPIE	Start with 10 lives—player 1	
6	ZANITPIE	Start with 10 lives—player 2	
7	AENASIPA	Never lose POW	

Remember that you can pick'n'mix your codes! You can enter up to THREE separate codes at one time.

Rush'N'Attack is a trademark of Konami Inc.
Game Genie is a trademark of Lewis Galoob Toys, Inc.

Section Z™ Game

Another game for which your Game Genie™ can offer infinite lives! Use Z Code 1 for infinite lives. Using Z Code 5 makes sure that your energy level gets boosted to full when you pick up an energy tube.

Z CODE	KEY IN . . .	EFFECT . . .	
1	SXOPUIVG	Infinite lives	

Some codes may cause undesired effects (which are not permanent). If this occurs,

2	PEXSIZLA	Start with 1 life
3	TEXSIZLA	Start with 6 lives
4	PEXSIZLE	Start with 9 lives
5	ZAUNUZAE	Energy tube gives full energy boost
6	NNNOUTSY	Autofiring capability

Remember that you can pick'n'mix your codes! You can enter up to THREE separate codes at one time.

Section Z is a trademark of Capcom USA, Inc.
Game Genie is a trademark of Lewis Galoob Toys, Inc.

Seicross™ Game

A real honcho could use SEI Code 5 to slow down all the movement, remembering that your energy still goes down at the same rate. That means that the power pick-ups are more distant from each other, and you have to be a better player to survive! Alternatively, use SEI Codes 2 thru 4 to adjust the number of lives that you start the game with. It's a real challenge with SEI Code 2!

SEI CODE	KEY IN . . .	EFFECT . . .
1	SUTEEX	Infinite lives
2	PELAGA	Start with 1 life
3	TELAGA	Start with 6 lives
4	PELAGE	Start with 9 lives
5	PEGEUG	Slow motion

Remember you can pick'n'mix your codes—you might want to use SEI Code 5 with one of the others to practice your funky stuff!

Seicross is a trademark of Nihon Bussan Co., Ltd.

Shadow of the Ninja™ Game

We've got bags of Codes to help (or hinder) you in battling Garuda™. If you wish to make the game harder, try SHAD Codes 3 and 7. If you need a bit of help, SHAD Codes 4 and 5 are the best.

SHAD CODE	KEY IN. . .	EFFECT . . .
1	SZSNIIVG	Infinite continues
2	PEEVZAIE	9 continues
3	PEEVZAIA	1 continue
4	GZVXSKSO	Don't lose energy from enemy attacks
5	AAVPGIGA	Don't lose energy from falling
6	APOEOGGA	Maximum energy gained from potion
7	PAOEOGGA	Less energy gained from potion
8	AZUAOGGO	40 throwing stars on pick-up
9	GPKAVGIA	20 bombs on pick-up

Shadow Of The Ninja and Garuda are trademarks of Natsume, Inc.

Shinobi™ Game

Sometimes even a ninja could use some more energy . . .try NOBI Code 6 to start with double your normal energy. If that's still not enough, NOBI Code 5 will give you infinite energy! You can also get a brilliant turbo-running ability if you use NOBI Code 7.

NOBI CODE	KEY IN . . .	EFFECT . . .	
1	SZEOLXVK	Infinite lives	
2	AANOLAZA	1 life	
3	IANOLAZA	6 lives	
4	AANOLAZE	9 lives	
5	SZNIPNVK	Infinite life energy	
6	GAXOTATE + GENPGPTE	Start with double normal energy	
7	IEKONILA	Turbo running	

Remember that you can pick'n'mix your codes! You can enter up to THREE separate codes at one time, or one double-code (like NOBI Code 6) and one single code (like NOBI Code 7).

Shinobi is a trademark of Sega Enterprises, Ltd.

Shooting Range™ Game

Along with a few Game Genie™ codes to make Shooting Range™ a lot easier, we also have some codes for crack shots to make the game harder—you can reduce the time allowed for each level, as well as reduce the bonus from shooting hourglasses (SHOO Code 11).

SHOO CODE	KEY IN . . .	EFFECT . . .	
1	ASUAIVAZ + ASXOVXAZ + SXVONOOU	Double usual shots per round	
2	ASUAIVAZ + ANXOVXAX + SXVONOOU	Triple usual shots per round	
3	ASUAIVAZ + EXXOVXAZ + SXVONOOU	Quadruple usual shots per round	
4	GEKAILLA + GAEETTLA	More time for level 1	
5	ZEKAILLA + ZAEETTLA	Less time for level 1	
6	GAOAATZA + AAOAPTZL	More time for level 2	
7	PAOAATZA + ZLOAPTZL	Less time for level 2	
8	GAOAZTZA + ZLOALTAA	More time for level 3	
9	PAOAZTZA + AAOALTAA	Less time for level 3	
10	GTEPOAZL	Double bonus time for hourglasses	
11	PPEPOAZU	Half bonus time for hourglasses	

Remember that you can pick'n'mix your codes!

Shooting Range is a trademark of Bandai America, Inc.
Game Genie is a trademark of Lewis Galoob Toys, Inc.

122

Some codes may cause undesired effects (which are not permanent). If this occurs,

Silent Service™ Game

For this adventure, Game Genie™ offers you extra gun shells, bow torpedoes and aft torpedoes. Try combining SIL Codes 2, 4, and 5 to really blast your way through enemy waters!

SIL

CODE	KEY IN . . .	EFFECT . . .	
1	ZLEPOIAI	Start with 50 deck gun shells	
2	LTEPOIAI	Start with 99 deck gun shells	
3	SZXVOPVG	Infinite deck gun shells	
4	SZSVUPVG	Infinite bow torpedoes	
5	SXETUPVG	Infinite aft torpedoes	

Remember that you can pick'n'mix your codes. You can enter up to THREE separate codes at one time.

Silent Service is a trademark of MicroProse Software Inc.

Game Genie is a trademark of Lewis Galoob Toys, Inc.

Silkworm™ Game

SILK Codes 20 and 21 restrict helicopter and jeep movement, giving less room to maneuver and making the game much more difficult. SILK Codes 12 thru 17 let you start on ANY level. And SILK Codes 18 and 19 let you keep your speed-ups and firepower!

SILK

CODE	KEY IN . . .	EFFECT . . .
1	PAXGXALA	Start with 1 life
2	TAXGXALA	Start with 6 lives
3	PAXGXALE	Start with 9 lives
4	SXSVIZVG	Infinite lives using helicopter
5	SZVVGTVG	Infinite lives using jeep
6	PEEGSPLA	1 life using helicopter after continue
7	TEEGSPLA	6 lives using helicopter after continue
8	PEEGSPLE	9 lives using helicopter after continue
9	PEOKNPLA	1 life using jeep after continue
10	TEOKNPLA	6 lives using jeep after continue
11	PEOKNPLE	9 lives using jeep after continue
12	PAXKEAAA	Start at stage 2
13	ZAXKEAAA	Start at stage 3
14	LAXKEAAA	Start at stage 4
15	GAXKEAAA	Start at stage 5
16	IAXKEAAA	Start at stage 6
17	TAXKEAAA	Start at stage 7
18	SZETZLSA	Keep firepower and speed-ups for helicopter
19	SXOTPTSA	Keep firepower and speed-ups for jeep
20	EEOVYUEI	Restrict movement area for helicopter
21	EEOVGYEV	Restrict movement area for jeep

Remember that you can pick'n'mix up to THREE separate codes in Silkworm!

Silkworm is a trademark of American Sammy Corp.

Silver Surfer™ Game

Silver Surfer™, have we got some great codes for you! SURF Codes 3 and 4 give players 1 and 2 a full supply of smart bombs from the start. SURF Code 5 gives you infinite lives and SURF Code 6 gives you infinite smart bombs. And with SURF Codes 7 and 8, losing a life doesn't mean you have to lose your collection of weapons!

SURF CODES	KEY IN . . .	EFFECT . . .	
1	PAOILIIA	1 life for player 1	
2	PAKSGIIA	1 life for player 2	
3	IAXSGIPA	Player 1 starts with 5 smart bombs	
4	IAVIIIPA	Player 2 starts with 5 smart bombs	
5	SXEKSNVK	Infinite lives for both players	
6	NYVTLVGO	Infinite smart bombs for both players	
7	GXEITSSE	Keep cosmic weapons after losing a life	
8	GXEILSSE + GXKIOUSE	Keep orbs after losing a life	
9	IEESIIPA	Have 5 smart bombs on a new life	

Remember that you can pick'n'mix your codes.

Silver Surfer is a trademark of Marvel Entertainment Group, Inc. Used by Arcadia Systems, Inc. under license.

The Simpsons™: Bart™ vs. The Space Mutants Game

Wow, some really excellent codes here! First there's mega-jump—it gives your high jump a super-boost, so reaching those difficult spots is now a cinch! BART Codes 2 thru 4 let you adjust the timer so you can have as much or as little time as you want to finish each level. And be sure to try out BART Code 7: Now when you buy things from shops, you won't get charged—there's no limit to how much equipment you can have! Pretty cool, huh?

BART CODE	KEY IN . . .	EFFECT . . .	
1	IPKYXUGA	Mega-jumping Bart!™	
2	XVONYXXK	Stop timer	
3	ANENPXGU	Slow down timer	
4	AXENPXGL	Speed up timer	
5	PAONAYAA	Gain 2 coins for every 1 collected	
6	PAONTNTE	Only 10 coins needed to get an extra life	
7	GXXZZOVK + GXXULEVK	Buy items for free!	

Remember that you can pick'n'mix your codes. You can enter up to THREE separate codes at one time or one double code (BART Code 7) and one single code (like BART Code 1).

The Simpsons and Bart are trademarks of Twentieth Century Fox Film Corporation. Used by Acclaim Entertainment, Inc. under license.

Some codes may cause undesired effects (which are not permanent). If this occurs,

Skate or Die 2™ Game

DIE Codes 1 thru 5 are for the Adventure Game, and DIE Codes 6 thru 13 work for the Stunt Ramp. DIE Code 1 protects you from any attacks, DIE Codes 2 thru 4 give you infinite ammo, and DIE Code 5 lets you really build up some speed for those jumps. DIE Code 9 provides infinite skateboards and DIE Code 12 gives you infinite time—you can perfect your stunts while building up an awesomely high score!

DIE CODE	KEY IN . . .	EFFECT . . .	
ADVENTURE GAME:			
1	SXUXZPVG	Infinite energy	
2	SXVPTVVK	Infinite paint clips	
3	AANPZPPA + AAXOZLPA	Infinite eggs	
4	AAVPTLPA + AEEOAPPA	Infinite M-80's	
5	AEESAAPG + AAKATAPG	Skate at any speed	
STUNT RAMP:			
6	PAUYLLLA	Only 1 skateboard	
7	TAUYLLLA	6 skateboards	
8	PAUYLLLE	9 skateboards	
9	SXKPVYVG + SXUZGAVG	Infinite skateboards	
10	TAONILLA	More time	
11	ZAONILLA	Less time	
12	SZUAKZVG	Stop timer	
13	TEKOKZIA	Super speed	

Remember that you can pick'n'mix your codes.

Skate or Die 2 is a trademark of Electronic Arts.

Skull & Crossbones™ Game

SKULL Codes 2 and 3 let you change the number of continues, and SKULL Codes 4 and 5 let you adjust your energy level to make the game harder or easier to suit your style. Be sure to check out SKULL Code 6—it gives 'super jump' a turbo-boost, and SKULL Code 7 provides non-stop blasting power!

SKULL CODES	KEY IN . . .	EFFECT . . .	
1	SZNOTNVK	Infinite continues	
2	PEXPTYIA	1 continue	
3	PEXPTYIE	9 continues	
4	POVPLYZU + POEPZYZU	Half energy for Red Dog™ and One Eye™	
5	LVVPLYZL + POEPZYZU	Double energy for Red Dog and One Eye	
6	EUVEYNEK + EUVAGNEK	Better super jump	
7	SUOEIVVS	Infinite weapons	

refer to pages 10 and 11 for instructions. If you still have problems, call 1-513-868-8835.

125

8	SZONGXVK	Stop timer	
9	AZONAXGL	Faster timer	
10	AYONAXGL	Slower timer	

Remember that you can pick'n'mix your codes.

Skull & Crossbones, Red Dog and One Eye are trademarks of Atari Games. Used by Tengen, Inc. under license.

Sky Kid™ Game

There are a whole bunch of level warps for this highly playable game—just try SKYK Codes 7 thru 10 to warp to a level you've never been to before. You can also play a friend who isn't as good as you—he or she should be player 1, and you should use SKYK Code 5 to give him or her more lives than you have.

SKYK
CODE	KEY IN . . .	EFFECT . . .	
1	SXEKGZVI	Infinite lives	
2	PANYNZLA	Start with 1 life—both players	
3	TANYNZLA	Start with 6 lives—both players	
4	PANYNZLE	Start with 9 lives—both players	
5	VANNVZSA	Player 1 has more lives than player 2	
6	AAOKIZPA	Shoot more bullets	
7	IAVNNZPA + GAVNUZAA	Start at level 5	
8	ZAVNNZPE + PAVNUZAE	Start at level 10	
9	APVNNZPA + YAVNUZAE	Start at level 15	
10	GPVNNZPA + LPVNUZAA	Start at level 20	

Remember that you can pick'n'mix your codes! You can enter up to THREE separate codes at one time, or one double-code (like SKYK Code 8) and one single code (like SKYK Code 1).

Sky Kid is a trademark of NAMCO Ltd.

Sky Shark™ Game

Use SKY Code 4 or 5 to disadvantage either player. SKY Codes 6 and 7 can be used to give an advantage to either player. Use SKY Codes 8 and 9 together to give yourself totally awesome power!

SKY
CODE	KEY IN . . .	EFFECT . . .	
1	OZNEAAVS	Infinite lives	
2	GXUEALVI	Infinite bombs	
3	GZNEIOVS	Infinite credits	
4	GZXATEOZ	Start with 1 life—player 1	
5	AAUALAGA	Start with 1 life—player 2	
6	TAXEZAXZ + PZXELENY	Start with 9 lives—player 1	
7	AAUALAGE	Start with 9 lives—player 2	
8	AAEELOGI	Autofire	
9	EZXAPPKZ + TAXAZOIL	Start with maximum firepower	

Some codes may cause undesired effects (which are not permanent). If this occurs,

10	TAVPSTLA	Double bombs	
11	TAUAYALA	Double credits	
12	AANEZPGA	1 life after continue—both players	
13	AANEZPGE	9 lives after continue—both players	

Remember that you can pick'n'mix your codes!

Sky Shark is a trademark of Taito America Corporation

Slalom™ Game

This great little skiing game is about to get harder: with SLALOM Code 1 you'll go hurtling down the slopes at a breakneck speed! However, if you prefer a gentler descent, try out SLALOM Codes 2 and 3.

SLALOM CODE	KEY IN . . .	EFFECT . . .	
1	PAOULZAA	Ski super fast!	
2	AAEPLIPA	No track obstacles	
3	XZXPATVZ + PAXPPVPN	Timer at 5 minutes for all tracks	

Slalom is a trademark of Nintendo of America & Rare Ltd.

Snake's Revenge™ Game

Look out dudes, 'cause man have we got some codes for you! There's SNAKE Codes 3 thru 7 for infinite blasting power, or try SNAKE Codes 8 thru 11 to start the game with your favorite weapon!

SNAKE CODE	KEY IN . . .	EFFECT . . .	
1	AXXVGYAG	Start with half bullets for Beretta M92	
2	EEXVGYAG	Start with double bullets for Beretta M92	
3	SZEEOUSE	Infinite Beretta ammo	
4	SXOASKSE	Infinite Shotgun ammo	
5	SZKAKKSE	Infinite Grenades	
6	SXVEOKSE	Infinite Missiles	
7	XTNTZVEE	Infinite ammo for all weapons	
8	ZEOVAYPA + XKXVTYEG	Start with Machine Gun instead of Beretta	
9	GEOVAYPA+ KKXVTYEG	Start with Shotgun instead of Beretta	
10	AXOVAYPA+ VKXVTYEG	Start with Grenades instead of Beretta	
11	EEOVAYPA+ EKXVTYEK	Start with Missiles instead of Beretta	

refer to pages 10 and 11 for instructions. If you still have problems, call 1-513-868-8835.

127

12	SXKVKASA	Infinite energy
13	XVUYTUZE + XTKZXKZE	Play with less energy
14	AEUVOAYA	Reduce your injuries by up to 50%

Remember that you can pick'n'mix codes. Enter up to THREE separate codes at one time. Or, try one double code (like SNAKE Code 8) and one single code (like SNAKE Code 14).

Snake's Revenge is a trademark of Ultra Software Corporation System.

Snake, Rattle 'N' Roll™ Game

Here's some codes to help those lovable snakes, Rattle™ and Roll,™ in this wacky 3-D adventure. There's a whole host of life codes, a fistful of level warps, plus super-jumps and mega-jumps to bounce you thru the game and up to those higher levels!

RAT
CODE   KEY IN ...   EFFECT ...

1	SXEYOZVG	Freeze timer
2	AGNNVXTT	Faster timer
3	EPNNVXTT	Slower timer
4	AEXAYZZA	1 life, both players
5	IEXAYZZA	6 lives, both players
6	AEXAYZZE	9 lives, both players
7	AEUAETZA	1 life, both players, after continue
8	IEUAETZA	6 lives, both players, after continue
9	AEUAETZE	9 lives, both players, after continue
10	PEUEGXNY	Start at level 2
11	ZEUEGXNY	Start at level 3
12	LEUEGXNY	Start at level 4
13	GEUEGXNY	Start at level 5
14	IEUEGXNY	Start at level 6
15	TEUEGXNY	Start at level 7
16	SLOUSVVS	Infinite lives, both players
17	ZAXOSGPA	Super jump
18	LAXOSGPA	Mega-jump

Remember that you can pick'n'mix your codes. You can enter up to THREE separate codes at one time.

Snake, Rattle n' Roll, Rattle and Roll are trademarks of Nintendo of America, Inc.

Soccer Game

SOC Codes 1 and 2 will change the length of each half—you can play more aggressively in a short game, or more tactically in a long one. SOC Codes 3 and 4 give player 1 an advantage, but your free goals won't show until you've scored your first goal.

SOC
CODE   KEY IN ...   EFFECT ...

| 1 | APOOKZIP | Each half lasts only 10 minutes |

Some codes may cause undesired effects (which are not permanent). If this occurs,

2	AIOOKZIP	Each half lasts for 50 minutes!
3	PASLVTAA + KASUOTSA + KASUUVSE	Player 1 starts 1 goal up
4	LASLVTAA + KASUOTSA + KASUUVSE	Player 1 starts 3 goals up

Remember that you can pick'n'mix your codes!

Solar Jetman™ Game

JET Codes 4 and 5 reduce the damage you get from hitting the cave walls—you'll be able to explore much further into the planets! JET Codes 6 thru 9 are level warps to help you find the passwords for the different levels, and then go back with more codes. JET Codes 13 thru 20 affect the gravity on each planet—some will make maneuvering your ship harder, but most will make it easier. If you lose your ship, your spaceman will be affected by the normal gravity of the planet.

JET CODE	KEY IN . . .	EFFECT . . .
1	PAKSZLGA	Only 1 ship and 1 life
2	AAKSZLGE	8 ships and 8 lives
3	SZXONIVG	Infinite lives
4	AEXXAVNY	Minimum damage taken from walls
5	AEXZGVSY + AEXXAVNY	No damage taken from walls
6	ZASSTLAA	Start on level 3
7	IASSTLAA	Start on level 6
8	AASSTLAE	Start on level 9
9	ZASSTLAE	Start on level 11
10	AASSZLPE	Start with more money
11	AEUIOXYA + GXKSOZSA	Items for free
12	SVEKOVON	Weapons use up no energy
13	UNSPLSLE	Reversed gravity for planet 1
14	VTSOZVTO	Reversed gravity for planet 2
15	KVOPATGP	Reversed gravity for planet 3
16	XNVOTSZE	Reversed gravity for planet 4
17	ETXPGTAZ	Reversed gravity for planet 5
18	OTUOYVPX	Reversed gravity for planet 6
19	UTEOPTLZ	Reversed gravity for planet 7
20	AOXOLVEV	Normal gravity for planet 8

Remember that you can pick'n'mix your codes.

Solar Jetman is a trademark of Rare Coin-It, Inc. Used by Tradewest, Inc. under license.

Solomon's Key™ Game

If you're having trouble solving this classic puzzle game, perhaps you need SOL Code 1—it'll give you infinite lives. If you've never managed to get very far, then try SOL Codes 7 thru 10 to warp to other levels, and also try SOL Code 3 to summon an army of fairies to help you beat the game!

SOL CODE	KEY IN . . .	EFFECT . . .	
1	XTKKKEXK	Infinite lives	
2	GZOXLAAX	Indestructible fireball	
3	AAXZIALZ	Continuous fairies	
4	KAXOOEVE	Start with 40,000 life points	
5	GZUPTOSE	Start on last level reached	
6	VTUPTOSE	Start on next level	
7	SZUOPOSE + UPUOLPGA + PAUPIPAE	Start on level 10	
8	SZUOPOSE + UPUOLPGA + LPUPIPAA	Start on level 20	
9	SZUOPOSE + UPUOLPGA + IPUPIPAE	Start on level 30	
10	SZUOPOSE + UPUOLPGA + YZUPIPAA	Start on level 40	

Remember that you can pick'n'mix your codes, although if you use any of the level warps you won't have room to enter any other codes!

Solomon's Key is a trademark of Tecmo, Inc.

Solstice™ Game

SOLS Codes 1 thru 5 give you a choice of lives. SOLS Code 6 gives you full magic powers right from the start of the game! And SOLS Code 9 gives you the power to jump when you're in the air, letting you hurdle right over almost all the enemies. It could also help you find your way into some 'hidden' rooms!

SOLS CODE	KEY IN . . .	EFFECT . . .	
1	SZSESXVK	Infinite lives	
2	PAKAVIGA	Start with 1 life	
3	AAKAVIGE	Start with 8 lives	
4	PAXELPLA	1 life after continue	
5	AAXELPLE	8 lives after continue	
6	GAOEUIZA	Start with full flasks of potions	
7	AAOEUIZA	Start with no potions	
8	SUSPIXVS	Never use up potions	
9	SXUXYGAX	Multi-jumping	

Remember that you can pick'n'mix your codes. You can enter up to THREE separate codes at one time.

Solstice is a trademark of Software Creations (ROM Developments) Ltd.

Spelunker™ Game

For all master Spelunker™ players, LUNK Code 5 is the one to try! It requires fine gaming skills and concentration, and a slightly twisted brain. On a more serious gaming level, you can give yourself protection against monsters, traps and falling from a great height. Use LUNK Code 6, but be careful not to get trapped!

Some codes may cause undesired effects (which are not permanent). If this occurs,

LUNK CODE	KEY IN . . .	EFFECT . . .	
1	IXOOPSVK	Infinite lives	
2	AANATPZA	Start with 1 life	
3	IANATPZA	Start with 6 lives	
4	AANATPZE	Start with 9 lives	
5	AEXAYTAP	Become invisible!	
6	ATKPAIAZ + TUEEYKNN + GXOAPKIX	Become invincible	

Remember that you can pick'n'mix your codes! You can enter up to THREE separate single codes at once, but LUNK Code 6 can only be entered on its own.
Spelunker is a trademark of Broderbund Software, Inc.

Spy Hunter™ Game

In this game you must score over 10,000 points to gain an extra car before the timer hits zero. The Game Genie™ has several ways of helping you combat this—you can slow up the timer, or even award yourself extra cars before you start! SPY Code 4 is useful too—you get to keep your special weapon after losing a car.

SPY CODE	KEY IN . . .	EFFECT . . .	
1	SXKAYOVK	Infinite lives	
2	SZKUANVK	Infinite missiles	
3	VXELTVSE	Infinite smoke	
4	GXSAKUSE + GXSANUSE	Keep special weapons	
5	ZEEXKIAA	Start with 2 extra lives	
6	TEEXKIAA	Start with 6 extra lives	
7	TEEXLILA	Double missiles on pick-up	
8	YAEZNIYE	Slow down timer	

Remember that you can pick'n'mix your codes! You can enter up to THREE separate codes at one time, or SPY Code 4 and one single code.
Spy Hunter is a trademark of Bally Midway Manufacturing Corp. Used by Sun Corporation of America under license.
Game Genie is a trademark of Lewis Galoob Toys, Inc.

Spy vs Spy™ Game

Aha! One of our very most favorite games—and here we have a big pile of codes for altering some of either spy's attributes. If you remember that the computer always plays the black spy in a one-player game, then you can really start cookin'! Try SPYS Code 6 to give yourself an awesome right hook!

SPYS CODE	KEY IN . . .	EFFECT . . .	
1	SZVAYUVK	Stop black spy's clock	
2	SXUELUVK	Stop white spy's clock	
3	PUEAPLIU	Black spy has 100 seconds in a minute	
4	PUSAILIU	White spy has 100 seconds in a minute	

| 5 | ONVZYNUT | Black spy has deadly punches |
| 6 | IEVZLYIE | White spy has deadly punches |

Remember, you can program your own codes! SPYS Codes 3 and 4 might make good codes to try your programming luck on!

Spy vs Spy is a trademark of EC Publications Inc. Used by Kemco-Seika Corporation under license.
Game Genie is a trademark of Lewis Galoob Toys, Inc.

Squoon™ Game

Use SQOO Codes 5 thru 7 to check out some later phases, but you might like to take along some extra lives—try SQOO Codes 3 and 4 for that! Fed up with waiting for your firepower? SQOO Code 10 gives you the main weapon the FIRST time you rescue some humans!

SQOO CODE	KEY IN . . .	EFFECT . . .	
1	AEEAAIPA	Infinite lives	
2	AEUESLZA	Start with 1 life	
3	IEUESLZA	Start with 6 lives	
4	AEUESLZE	Start with 9 lives	
5	LASEXLPA	Start at phase 3	
6	IASEXLPA	Start at phase 5	
7	AASEXLPE	Start at phase 8	
8	GXEAKKSE + GXSUZXSE	Never lose humans on dying	
9	SZEEOSVK	Never lose your special weapon	
10	ZEOOEYPA	Gain main weapon on rescuing 9 humans	

Remember that you can use up to THREE separate codes at one time with your Game Genie™—the ultimate mix for this game is SQOO Codes 8 and 9.

Sqoon is a trademark of IREM Corp.
Game Genie is a trademark of Lewis Galoob Toys, Inc.

Star Soldier™ Game

Try STAR Codes 1 and 2 together for mega power. STAR Code 2 gives you a laser weapon that's not usually available—how's that for style? Gee, thanks, Game Genie™!

STAR CODE	KEY IN . . .	EFFECT . . .	
1	SZOEAPVG	Infinite lives	
2	PEOAPPAA	Start with laser	
3	GXVPXTVG	Infinite shield power	
4	ZAOOOYIE + ZENOGLIE	Double shield power	

Remember that you can pick'n'mix your codes!

Star Soldier is a trademark of Hudson Soft USA, Inc.
Game Genie is a trademark of Lewis Galoob Toys, Inc.

Star Voyager™ Game

The life support pods are important to the survival of you and your ship—once all the pods have gone, you die! Luckily, with the Game Genie™ you can choose the number of pods you have using VOY Codes 1 thru 3. Also, because power equipment is extremely important to your survival, we've rigged it so that you can stop your equipment from taking any damage using

Some codes may cause undesired effects (which are not permanent). If this occurs,

VOY Codes 4 thru 7.

VOY CODE	KEY IN . . .	EFFECT . . .	
1	GZSZSTVG	Infinite life support pods	
2	GPKIASZA	Start with double life support pods	
3	TPKIASZE	Start with triple life support pods	
4	AASLSLLA	Barrier won't take damage	
5	AOKLVLEI	Radar won't take damage	
6	ENXLXLEI	Cannon won't take damage	
7	AAXUXLLA	Engine won't take damage	

Remember that you can pick'n'mix your codes! You might want to choose three from VOY Codes 4 thru 7 to protect strategic parts of your ship.

Star Voyager is a trademark of Acclaim Entertainment, Inc.
Game Genie is a trademark of Lewis Galoob Toys, Inc.

Starforce™ Game

FORCE Code 5 really makes this game a lot more challenging for expert gamers, while beginners should try FORCE Codes 3 and 4, and if they still can't cut it, FORCE Code 1.

FORCE CODE	KEY IN . . .	EFFECT . . .	
1	SZKEVTVG	Infinite lives	
2	AEUAUIZA	Start with 1 life	
3	IEUAUIZA	Start with 6 lives	
4	AEUAUIZE	Start with 9 lives	
5	VYVEGONN	Turbo speed	

Remember that you can pick'n'mix your codes—you might like to try FORCE Code 5 in combination with any one of the others.

Starforce is a trademark of Tecmo, Inc.

Starship Hector™ Game

For Starship Hector™ we have extra lives and stage warps to let you explore further into the game. HEC Code 5 gives you four times the energy when you pick up capsules, and HEC Code 6 gives you some handy protection against those bio-mechanical nasties!

HEC CODE	KEY IN . . .	EFFECT . . .	
1	SZKIOGVG	Infinite lives	
2	AANSOGZA	Start with 1 life	
3	IANSOGZA	Start with 6 lives	
4	AANSOGZE	Start with 9 lives	
5	GEVVGIPA	Extra energy from capsules	
6	OVUYEGSV + PEUYOGTA	Take minimum damage	

refer to pages 10 and 11 for instructions. If you still have problems, call 1-513-868-8835.

133

7	PENYGIAA	Start at stage 2
8	ZENYGIAA	Start at stage 3
9	LENYGIAA	Start at stage 4
10	GENYGIAA	Start at stage 5

Remember that you can pick'n'mix your codes. Enter up to THREE separate codes at one time or HEC Code 6 and one single code (like HEC Code 9).

Starship Hector is a trademark of Hudson Soft USA, Inc.

Stealth ATF™ Game

Well, a motley crew of Game Genie™ codes for Stealth ATF™ . . .

ATF CODE	KEY IN . . .	EFFECT . . .
1	SZVZSSVK	Infinite missiles
2	AOUXXEAA	Start with double missiles
3	SZVPXNVV	No damage taken from enemy's bullets
4	AVUXNAVP	Start with less fuel
5	AEKZZLZE	More enemy planes on the screen

Remember that you can pick'n'mix your codes! You can enter up to THREE separate codes into your Game Genie™ at one time.

Stealth ATF is a trademark of Activision, Inc.
Game Genie is a trademark of Lewis Galoob Toys, Inc.

Stinger™ Game

Can you save Earth from being turned into a ball of cotton candy?! Well, for this mega-mission we have prepared some most excellent codes! Use STING Codes 6 thru 14 for mega fighting power and STING Codes 15 thru 18 for as many lives as it takes!
NOTE: WHEN USING STING CODES 1 THRU 5 YOU MUST WAIT FOR THE DEMO TO START BEFORE PLAYING THE GAME.

STING CODE	KEY IN . . .	EFFECT . . .
1	GZOGIGSA + PAEGPLPA	Start at stage 2
2	GZOGIGSA + ZAEGPLPA	Start at stage 3
3	GZOGIGSA + LAEGPLPA	Start at stage 4
4	GZOGIGSA + GAEGPLPA	Start at stage 5
5	GZOGIGSA + IAEGPLPA	Start at stage 6
6	YGNGAKTL + PAVKTGAP	Start with Dual Cannons
7	YGNGAKTL + ZAVKTGAP	Start with Laser
8	YGNGAKTL + GAVKTGAP	Start with Shoot Right
9	YGNGAKTL + AAVKTGAO	Start with Shoot Left
10	YGNGAKTL + APVKTGAP	Start with Five Direction Firing
11	YGNGAKTL + AZVKTGAP	Start with Three Direction Firing
12	YGNGAKTL + AGVKTGAP	Start with Force field
13	YGNGAKTL + EAVKTGAP	Start with 2 Extra Stingers
14	GZNGNLSP	Keep weapons after death

Some codes may cause undesired effects (which are not permanent). If this occurs,

15	PAXKPGLA	Start with 1 life
16	TAXKPGLA	Start with 6 lives
17	PAXKPGLE	Start with 9 lives
18	OZVKKLVS	Infinite lives

Stinger is a trademark of Konami Inc.

Street Cop™ Game

Need a hand catching those bad dudes? Game Genie™ is here to save the day! Adjust the timer and energy bar to your advantage with COP Codes 2 and 7. If you want to see those later stages, check-out COP Codes 8 thru 10.

COP CODE	KEY IN . . .	EFFECT . . .	
1	TAOVTXPA	Less time on the timer	
2	ZPOVTXPA	More time on the timer	
3	SZSNTAVG	Stop timer	
4	GXESTZST	Immune to damage	
5	OVESTZSV + PEESYZAP	Take minimum damage	
6	AONGNAAU	Start with less energy	
7	AVNGNAAL	Start with more energy	
8	PAXTPPAA	Start at level 2	
9	ZAXTPPAA	Start at level 3	
10	LAXTPPAA	Start at level 4	

Remember that you can pick'n'mix codes. Enter up to THREE separate codes at one time, or one double code (COP Code 5) and one single code (like COP Code 2).

Street Cop is a trademark of Bandai America, Inc.
Game Genie is a trademark of Lewis Galoob Toys, Inc.

Street Fighter 2010: The Final Fight™ Game

Street Fighter™ fans, check out FIGHT Code 4—you can now become invincible! You can also have 9 lives with FIGHT Code 2, or infinite lives with FIGHT Code 3. FIGHT Code 7 keeps you from losing your power-ups when you lose a life, and FIGHT Code 8 keeps you from losing them when you get hit. (NOTE: any power-ups above three will be lost when you get hit.)

FIGHT CODE	KEY IN . . .	EFFECT . . .	
1	AAEETAGA	Start with 1 life	
2	PAEETAGE	Start with 9 lives	
3	SZUATPVG	Infinite lives	
4	AEUIPGZA	Become invincible!	
5	PEUIPGZA	Take less damage	
6	LEUIPGZA	Take more damage	
7	GZOAZPSA	Keep power-ups after losing a life	
8	AEKIYGZA	Keep power-ups when hit	
9	ZESESPPA	Faster Ken™	

refer to pages 10 and 11 for instructions. If you still have problems, call 1-513-868-8835.

135

Remember that you can pick'n'mix your codes.

Street Fighter 2010: the Final Fight and Ken are trademarks of Capcom U.S.A., Inc.

Strider™ Game

If you're having some difficulty, look no further than your Game Genie™! STRI Codes 1 and 2 give you more attack energy, which is crucial for Strider's™ tricks. STRI Codes 3 and 4 give Strider a little health boost . . .useful in sticky situations!

STRI CODE	KEY IN . . .	EFFECT . . .	
1	ZAUXEYPE	More energy from small capsules (10)	
2	GPUXXNZA	More energy from big capsules (20)	
3	ZAUXKYPE	Health from small capsules (10)	
4	GPUXVNZA	Health from big capsules (20)	
5	ZAEXVNAO	Double health and energy from all capsules	

Strider is a trademark of Capcom.
Game Genie is a trademark of Lewis Galoob Toys, Inc.

Super C™ Game

Here it is, the mission to end all missions! There's a choice of lives with SUPER Codes 1 thru 3. Or you can fight for your lives by using SUPER Code 13, which gives you a bonus life every time you shoot an enemy soldier. Why not have a look at those later stages with SUPER Codes 7 thru 12?

SUPER CODE	KEY IN . . .	EFFECT . . .	
1	AEXTLIZA	1 life for both players	
2	IEXTLIZA	6 lives for both players	
3	AEXTLIZE	9 lives for both players	
4	EUUTGIYS + YSXTPSEL + ZEUTZIAA	Start game with Spray Gun	
5	EUUTGIYS + YSXTPSEL + GEUTZIAA	Start game with Fireball Gun	
6	SPVAZTGZ	Keep weapon after losing a life	
7	PEETLIAA	Start at area 2	
8	ZEETLIAA	Start at area 3	
9	LEETLIAA	Start at area 4	
10	GEETLIAA	Start at area 5	
11	IEETLIAA	Start at area 6	
12	TEETLIAA	Start at area 7	
13	AENTTTZA	Bonus life for each enemy soldier shot	
14	TEEVIIZA	9 continues	
15	SZOVXZVG	Infinite continues	

Remember that you can pick'n'mix your codes.

Super C is a trademark of Konami Inc.

Some codes may cause undesired effects (which are not permanent). If this occurs,

Super Mario Bros.™ Game

A super game with a super selection of codes! Check them out!

SMB
CODE   KEY IN . . .   EFFECT . . .

LIVES!

Codes 1 to 5 let you adjust lives. Code 4 is really good for handicapping one player.

1	AATOZA	Start players 1 & 2 with 1 life
2	IATOZA	Start players 1 & 2 with 6 lives
3	AATOZE	Start players 1 & 2 with 9 lives
4	VATOLE	Start player 1 with 8 lives and player 2 with 3 lives
5	SXIOPO	Infinite lives for both players

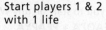
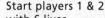

JUMPS!

Super and Mega-jumps can be achieved while standing still, running or turbo running (holding down button B). Try entering Codes 6, 7 and 8 or Codes 9, 10 and 11 for all-around Super- or Mega-jumping.

Super jumps let you jump better—the effect is especially noticeable when turbo running.

6	APZLGK	Super jump from a standing start only
7	TPZLTG	Super jump from running only
8	GPZUAG	Super jump from turbo running only

Mega-jumps enable you to jump almost to the top of the screen—right off the top when turbo running!

9	APZLGG	Mega-jump from a standing start only
10	APZLTG	Mega-jump from running only
11	GAZUAG	Mega-jump from turbo running only

MOON GRAVITY!

Moon Gravity is a brilliant ability! It has weird and wonderful effects. Again, it works when stationary, running, or turbo running. The Moon Gravity effect is more fun than Super- or Mega-jumps, but it is harder to get used to. Stay with it and you'll find that it gives the game an added twist!

You can control the height of your Moon jumps. To jump really high, tap button A really quickly. To do low jumps hold down button A for about one second.

Use this power to find new places to explore. You can even jump over the flags! (If you're playing to complete the game rather than just explore it, don't jump over the flagpoles—or else you'll get "stuck" and have to reset.)

12	YAZULG	Moon Gravity from a standing start
13	YAZUIG	Moon Gravity from a running start

refer to pages 10 and 11 for instructions. If you still have problems, call 1-513-868-8835.

14	YAZUYG	Moon Gravity from turbo running only

STAY BIG!
Code 15 will keep you big. However, you can still die if you fall down holes.

15	OZTLLX + AATLGZ + SZLIVO	Always stay big

WORLDWARPING!
Codes 16 to 22 allow you to start on any World of your choice!

16	YSAOPE + YEAOZA + PEAPYA	Start on World 2
17	YSAOPE + YEAOZA + ZEAPYA	Start on World 3
18	YSAOPE + YEAOZA + LEAPYA	Start on World 4
19	YSAOPE + YEAOZA + GEAPYA	Start on World 5
20	YSAOPE + YEAOZA + IEAPYA	Start on World 6
21	YSAOPE + YEAOZA + TEAPYA	Start on World 7
22	YSAOPE + YEAOZA + YEAPYA	Start on World 8

Super Mario Bros. is a trademark of Nintendo of America Inc.

Super Mario Bros.™ 2 Game

Super Mario Brothers™ 2 has a world of Codes! SMB2 Codes 1 and 2 together give you immense power. SMB2 Codes 28 to 33 let you select which world you start on. SMB2 Code 7 is sure to be a favorite—it's just like flying!

SMB2 CODE	KEY IN . . .	EFFECT . . .
1	SZNESXVK	Infinite lives
2	GZELVXSE	Infinite life meter (except if you hit a spike)
3	GOEANKAO + USEEEKKA	Walk backwards
4	SXUASXOU	Quick pick up
5	AEUEKKGL	Special "squat" high jumps
6	PPXAOIAA	Princess has mega-float
7	PAXAOIAA	Princess has mega-float and lunar descent
8	PESEGLGA	Super moonjumps for Mario™
9	AAEEZGPA	Mega moonjumps for Luigi™
10	PENALLGA	Super moonjumps for Toad™
11	PAXAPGGA	Super moonjumps for Princess™
12	XVVANSZK + XVNEXSZV	Super turbo running
13	AEVAVIIA + AENEEITA	Permanent turbo running
14	AXSETUAO + ESVAPUEV	Super fast run for Mario

Some codes may cause undesired effects (which are not permanent). If this occurs,

15	AZEEGKAO + EIEEYKEV	Super fast run for Luigi	
16	AXNAIUAO + ESNEAUEV	Fast run for Toad	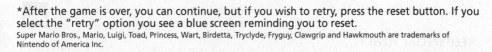
17	AZXALKAO + EIXATKEV	Super fast run for Princess	
18	AEXALGZA	Speed up enemies	
19	AXNAZSAA + EVNALSEY	Super speed enemies	

NOTE: There are two versions given for some of the following Codes. If one code doesn't work on your game, then try the alternate Code.

20	YESUAPTE / YESLPPTE	Strong Wart™	
21	IAVENYZE / IAVEUYZE	Strong Birdetta™	
22	YAXXIYZE	Strong Tryclyde™	
23	YAVXVGGE	Strong Fryguy™	
24	YAEXTPGE	Strong Clawgrip™	
25	YEVXVYLE / YEVZNYLE	Strong Hawkmouth™	
26	AAVENYZA / AAVEUYZA	Weak Birdetta	
27	TPEPLAAX / TONENYAX	Birdetta spits eggs instead of fireballs (appears in late levels of the game)	
28	PEEPUZAG + IUEPSZAA + TEEPVZPA	Start on World 2 *	
29	ZEEPUZAG + IUEPSZAA + TEEPVZPA	Start on World 3 *	
30	LEEPUZAG + IUEPSZAA + TEEPVZPA	Start on World 4 *	
31	GEEPUZAG + IUEPSZAA + TEEPVZPA	Start on World 5 *	
32	IEEPUZAG + IUEPSZAA + TEEPVZPA	Start on World 6 *	
33	TEEPUZAG + IUEPSZAA + TEEPVZPA	Start on World 7 *	

*After the game is over, you can continue, but if you wish to retry, press the reset button. If you select the "retry" option you see a blue screen reminding you to reset.

Super Mario Bros., Mario, Luigi, Toad, Princess, Wart, Birdetta, Tryclyde, Fryguy, Clawgrip and Hawkmouth are trademarks of Nintendo of America Inc.

Super Mario Bros.™ 3 Game

All the Mario™ addicts will be pleased to see the powerful Game Genie™ codes that we've collected for the latest Mario adventure—41 codes in all! SMB3 Code 1 is obviously a good one. SMB3 Codes 4 thru 12 are really great fun, and SMB3 Codes 14 to 20 let you explore the whole of Mario Land™!

SMB3 CODE	KEY IN . . .	EFFECT . . .	
1	SLXPLOVS	Infinite lives for Mario™ and Luigi™	
2	AEKPTZGA	1 life for Mario and Luigi after continue	
3	AEKPTZGE	9 lives for Mario and Luigi after continue	

refer to pages 10 and 11 for instructions. If you still have problems, call 1-513-868-8835.

139

SUPER JUMPS

4	ELKZYVEK	Power Jumps
5	EZKZYVEK	Super Power Jumps
6	EAKZYVEK	Mega Power Jumps
7	LEKZNGIE	Mega Moon Jumps
8	GZUXNGEI	Multi-Jumps
9	SXEZSKOZ	Skywalker

STAR CODES! (these codes work really well together)

10	OXKZELSX	Super speed running
11	XVUXNUEE	Turbocharged running
12	SEUZELSZ	"Stop-on-a-dime"

POWER "TAKE OFF" METER

| 13 | AANZKLLA | Can raise power meter while standing still so that you can fly from a standing start |

START ON ANY WORLD

14	PEUZUGAA	Start on World 2
15	ZEUZUGAA	Start on World 3
16	LEUZUGAA	Start on World 4
17	GEUZUGAA	Start on World 5
18	IEUZUGAA	Start on World 6
19	TEUZUGAA	Start on World 7
20	YEUZUGAA	Start on World 8

RE-USE ITEMS!

| 21 | YPXXLVGE | Mario (not Luigi) can re-use items again and again |

KEEP SPECIAL POWERS

| 22 | SZUEXNSO | Restore powers after playing an action scene (e.g. if you were "Fire Mario™" on the map screen, then entered an action scene, died or changed to "Frog Mario™," you would return to the map scene as "Fire Mario") |

SELECT SUPER ABILITY

The following codes are useful with Code 22.

23	ZEUXKGAA	Start the game as Fire Mario
24	LEUXKGAA	Start the game as Raccoon Mario™
25	GEUXKGAA	Start the game as Frog Mario
26	IEUXKGAA	Start the game as Tanooki Mario™
27	TEUXKGAA	Start the game as 'Sledgehammer' Mario™!

Some codes may cause undesired effects (which are not permanent). If this occurs,

SELECT PERMANENT SUPER ABILITY

IMPORTANT: IF YOU USE ANY OF CODES 28 THRU 32 TO DEFEAT BOWZER™, YOU SHOULD STAND IN FRONT OF THE DOOR AND HOLD "UP." AS SOON AS THE DOOR OPENS, YOU WILL PASS THROUGH INTO THE CHAMBER WHERE THE PRINCESS IS HELD. IF YOU DO NOT DO THIS, YOU MAY GET CAUGHT IN BOWZER'S TIME TRAP AND THE GAME WILL PAUSE FOREVER!

28	XUKXGLIE	Start and stay as Super Mario™
29	UXKXGLIA	Start and stay as Fire Mario
30	NXKXGLIE	Start and stay as Raccoon Mario™!
31	OUKXGLIE	Start and stay as Frog Mario
32	XNKXGLIE	Start and stay as Sledgehammer Mario™

INVINCIBILITY

| 33 | SZKIKXSE | Invincibility after changing up from Super Mario (e.g. to Raccoon, Frog, etc.) |

AUTOMATIC SUPER ABILITY AFTER YOU FALL AND DIE
With all of the following codes, you will find that you change into Super Mario if you die again:

34	AEOSSZPA + PAOZTGAA	Change to SUPER MARIO if you fall off screen and die
35	AEOSSZPA + ZAOZTGAA	Change to FIRE MARIO if you fall off screen and die
36	AEOSSZPA + LAOZTGAA	Change to RACCOON MARIO if you fall off screen and die
39	AEOSSZPA + GAOZTGAA	Change to FROG MARIO if you fall off screen and die
40	AEOSSZPA + IAOZTGAA	Change to TANOOKI MARIO if you fall off screen and die
41	AEOSSZPA + TAOZTGAA	Change to SLEDGEHAMMER MARIO if you fall off screen and die

All codes (except as noted) work for Luigi as well as Mario.

Remember that you can pick'n'mix your codes! You can enter up to three of the 8-letter codes at one time, but certain effects will need more than one of these codes to work. Have fun, and remember to try Sledgehammer Mario—he's rock hard!

Super Mario Bros., Mario, Mario Land, Luigi, Fire Mario, Raccoon Mario, Frog Mario, Tanooki Mario, Sledgehammer Mario, Super Mario and Bowzer are trademarks of Nintendo of America Inc.
Game Genie is a trademark of Lewis Galoob Toys, Inc.

Super Pitfall™ Game

Lots and lots of juicy Game Genie™ codes for this one—these codes are particularly suited to stacking the game in favor of one of the players. We also have the usual infinite lives and infinite bullets codes for those who want them—pick 'em, mix 'em, you'll be able to kick 'em!

PIT CODE	KEY IN . . .	EFFECT . . .	
1	SZKSASVK	Infinite lives—1-player game	
2	SXESTSVK	Infinite lives—player 1	
3	SXXSZSVK	Infinite lives—player 2	

refer to pages 10 and 11 for instructions. If you still have problems, call 1-513-868-8835.

4	PAVIPALA	Both players start with 1 life
5	TAVIPALA	Both players start with 6 lives
6	PAVIPALE	Both players start with 9 lives
7	LEXKNYZA	Start with 30 bullets
8	PEXKNYZA	Start with 10 bullets
9	AEOYILPA	Infinite bullets
10	LENLELZA	30 bullets gained on pick-up
11	PENLELZA	10 bullets gained on pick-up

Remember that you can pick'n'mix your codes! You can enter up to THREE separate codes at one time.

Super Pitfall is a trademark of Activision, Inc.
Game Genie is a trademark of Lewis Galoob Toys, Inc.

Super Sprint™ Game

With the help of your Game Genie™, you can get extra continue options and increase the occurence of obstacles on the track. If you want the game to be more challenging—try SPRI Code 6.

SPRI CODE	KEY IN . . .	EFFECT . . .
1	SZETVUVK	Infinite continues
2	YASSPALA	6 continues
3	PASSPALA	No continues
4	IEKKNTAA + GXSGUVSE	More obstacles on tracks
5	ZEKKNTAE + GXSGUVSE	Even more obstacles on tracks
6	YEKKNTAE + GXSGUVSE	Lots and lots of obstacles on tracks

Remember that you can pick'n'mix your codes! You can enter up to THREE separate codes at one time, or one double-code (like SPRI Code 4) and one single code (like SPRI Code 3).

Super Sprint is a trademark of Atari Games Corporation. Used by Tengen under license.
Game Genie is a trademark of Lewis Galoob Toys, Inc.

Superman™ Game

Even the original superhero can find the Game Genie™ useful. You can make sure that you never run out of super power with SUPER Code 2, and start with an advantage by using SUPER Codes 3 and 4. There's also a bunch of level warps (SUPER Codes 7 through 10) but remember that you won't be able to use other SUPER Codes with them because they each use all three Game Genie™ "wishes."

SUPER CODE	KEY IN . . .	EFFECT . . .
1	AAXSEIEA	Never die when out of super power
2	SXNSSKSE	Never lose super power
3	XVUVYZIA	Start with lots of super power
4	AVEOUIAL	Double max power of all items at start

Some codes may cause undesired effects (which are not permanent). If this occurs,

5	AXUPYLAP	Double usual item power on item power crystal pick-up
6	EXUPYLAP	Full item power on item power crystal pick-up
7	EZVPKSOZ + PAVPSIAA + KANPXSSE	Start at mission 2
8	EZVPKSOZ + ZAVPSIAA + KANPXSSE	Start at mission 3
9	EZVPKSOZ + LAVPSIAA + KANPXSSE	Start at mission 4
10	EZVPKSOZ + GAVPSIAA + KANPXSSE	Start at mission 5

Remember that you can pick'n'mix your codes! You can enter one mission warp or up to THREE other codes at one time.

Superman is a trademark of DC Comics Inc. Used by Kemco Seika Corp. under license.
Game Genie is a trademark of Lewis Galoob Toys, Inc.

Swords & Serpents™ Game

When you create an 'all new adventure party', be sure to use SWORD Codes 1 thru 3. SWORD Codes 1 and 2 give each new character extra health points and SWORD Code 3 gives everyone Scale Armor! SWORD Codes 4 thru 11 all improve the powers of the different characters in your party—try them out and see which ones you like best!

SWORD CODE	KEY IN . . .	EFFECT . . .
1	TPXGNVZE + TPXKSVZE	Start with 30 health points each
2	ZLXGNVZA + ZLXKSVZA	Start with 50 health points each
3	VANGKTVE	All characters have Scale Armor
4	UEEKSTOE	Warriors start with a Great Sword
5	KEEKSTOE	Warriors start with a Great Axe
6	SEEGETSE	Magicians start with a Wizard's Wand
7	YPKGSTLE	Magicians start with more spells
8	LAKKXTAA	Magicians have greater spells
9	GZKYLGOY	Spells use up no magic points
10	XEOGVTXE	Thieves start with a Long Sword
11	KEOGVTXA	Thieves start with an Axe

Remember that you can pick'n'mix your codes. You can enter up to THREE separate codes at one time or one double code (like SWORD Code 2) and one single code (like SWORD Code 4).

Swords and Serpents is a trademark of Acclaim Entertainment, Inc.

T & C Surf Designs™ Game

Here's some crucially cool codes to help you become the ultimate surf 'n skate champion! SURF Code 6 lets you increase the playing time, and SURF Code 5 stops the timer altogether! SURF Codes 3 and 4 make sure that you lose fewer symbols if you make any mistakes.

SURF CODE	KEY IN . . .	KEY IN . . .
1	GXUZZZVG	Infinite lives for skating
2	GXNKALVG	Infinite lives for surfing
3	PEOGILZA	When surfing lose only 1 symbol

---

refer to pages 10 and 11 for instructions. If you still have problems, call 1-513-868-8835.

4	PAEZYALA	When skating lose only 1 symbol if you fall into the ocean or a crack	
5	GXKLXAVG	Stop timer	
6	LESPGZPA	Increase time	

T & C Surf Designs is a trademark of Town & Country Surf Shop Inc. Used by LJN Toys, Ltd. under license.

Target: Renegade™ Game

Lots of Game Genie™ goodies for Target: Renegade™! You can reduce the amount of damage that your enemies do to you by using TAR Codes 5 and 6. There are also a whole bunch of level warps (TAR Codes 7 thru 12), and some codes to alter the timer and even freeze it altogether (see TAR Codes 1 thru 3).

TAR CODE	KEY IN . . .	EFFECT . . .	
1	SZEAOZVG	Freeze timer	
2	SXEATXSU	Set timer to 5:00 for all levels	
3	SXEATXSU + NKEEAZEE	Set timer to 3:00 for all levels	
4	AEKESZZA	Hearts replenish energy to maximum	
5	SXVZVTSA	Don't take most damage	
6	TASPSPGP	Take half damage from bosses	
7	PAOOYZAA	Start on level 2	
8	ZAOOYZAA	Start on level 3	
9	LAOOYZAA	Start on level 4	
10	GAOOYZAA	Start on level 5	
11	IAOOYZAA	Start on level 6	
12	TAOOYZAA	Start on level 7	

Remember that you can pick'n'mix your codes! You can enter up to THREE separate codes at one time, or TAR Code 3 and one other TAR code.

Target: Renegade is a trademark of Ocean Software Ltd.
Game Genie is a trademark of Lewis Galoob Toys, Inc.

Tecmo Bowl™ Game

BOWL Code 1 gives both teams only two downs, making gameplay fast and furious. BOWL Code 2 gives you six downs, giving you more chances to score when you're on offense. And BOWL Code 3 lengthens the 1st Quarter to 4 1/2 minutes playing time.

BOWL CODE	KEY IN . . .	EFFECT . . .	
1	ZAXAYIGA + ZAXOTPGA	Only 2 downs allowed	
2	TAXAYIGA + TAXOTPGA	6 downs allowed	
3	GAOATSPA	More time for the 1st Quarter	

Tecmo Bowl is a trademark of Tecmo, Inc.

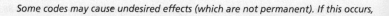

Teenage Mutant Ninja Turtles™ Game

All right! Strap that shell on your back and let's get into some serious code-play . . . TEEN Codes 1 and 2 let you choose how many weapons you get, and TEEN Code 4 makes sure you don't take damage from most things. There's a code for getting your energy restored to max every time you eat pizza (TEEN Code 6) and a couple to deal with the lengthy issue of the rope . . .(sorry, that wasn't funny, was it?).

TEEN CODE	KEY IN . . .	EFFECT . . .	
1	ZENOATGO	Pick up 10 weapons only	
2	ZUNOATGP	Pick up 50 weapons at a time!	
3	SZNVZAVI	Keep weapons (but can't be used with TEEN Codes 1 and 2!)	
4	GXSOUAST	Don't take most damage	
5	SXVZGSOO	Don't take damage from seaweed	
6	AEOOGTZA	Full energy boost from pizza slices	
7	GPUOLNZA	20 missiles on pick-up	
8	TAKOPYLA	Double rope on pick-up	
9	SXVXTLVG	Never lose rope	

Remember that you can pick'n'mix your codes!
Teenage Mutant Ninja Turtles is a trademark of Mirage Studios, USA. Used by Ultra Software Corp. under license.

Teenage Mutant Ninja Turtles™ II: The Arcade Game™

Yo! These here codes are like mucho radical! Pick your favorite goon-ripping attack mode and make it even more awesome with TMNT2 Codes 5, 6 or 8! Or, get extra lives with TMNT2 Codes 2 or 3. If you're using TMNT2 Code 10, remember one of you must have a spare life for this code to take effect.

TMNT2 CODE	KEY IN . . .	EFFECT . . .	
1	PEOIAPZA	Start with 1 life	
2	TEOIAPZA	Start with 6 lives	
3	PEOIAPZE	Start with 9 lives	
4	AAEAULPA	Infinite lives	
5	PEXTKZZE	More powerful turtle weapon	
6	PEOVKZGE	More powerful 'jump + attack'	
7	ZEOVKZGA	Weaker 'jump + attack'	
8	PEXTEZLE	More powerful kick	
9	PEXTEZLA	Weaker kick	
10	SXEAPZVG + SZUAYZVG	In two-turtle mode, when one player is revived the other player's spare life won't get used up	

Remember that you can pick'n'mix your codes. You can enter up to THREE separate codes at one time, or one double (TMNT2 Code 10) and one single (like TMNT2 Code 8).

refer to pages 10 and 11 for instructions. If you still have problems, call 1-513-868-8835.

If you want to try altering codes, TMNT2 Codes 5, 6 and 8 are goods ones to use. See the section about programming your own codes at the front of the Codebook for some useful hints.

Teenage Mutant Ninja Turtles II and The Arcade Game are trademarks of Mirage Studios, U.S.A. Used by Ultra Software Corporation under license.

Terra Cresta™ Game

TERA Code 5 is fab! After entering TERA Code 5 you can split and reform your ship as many times as you like. TERA Code 8 is also great—it gives you a secret mega-weapon which is not usually available! For a heavy blasting session try TERA Code 7, which makes you immune to any damage!

TERA CODE	KEY IN . . .	EFFECT . . .	
1	SZKVPTVG	Infinite lives	
2	AAKSPGZA	Start with 1 life	
3	IAKSPGZA	Start with 6 lives	
4	AAKSPGZE	Start with 9 lives	
5	SXSTULVG	Infinite "ship formation" splits	
6	PEOTEALE + PEKGETLE	9 "ship formation" splits	
7	KTKSLGAZ	Indestructible!	
8	AEVKNYLA	A secret mega-weapon	

Remember that you can pick'n'mix your codes—you can enter up to THREE at once, or TERA Code 6 and any one of the others.

Terra Cresta is a trademark of Vic Tokai, Inc.

Tetris™ Game

TET Code 5 makes the blocks fall down the screen faster when you press DOWN on your joypad, but the real star of the codes for this game must be TET Code 1. That's right, you can now play two-player Tetris™! Player 1 controls the rotation and player 2 controls the left and right movement of the blocks. To make a block fall fast, player 2 must press DOWN, and then player 1 must press DOWN. It's incredibly good fun, and a great test of how well two players can communicate—try it!

TET CODE	KEY IN . . .	EFFECT . . .	
1	ENEALYNN	Two-player interactive game!	
2	APSEGYIZ	Need only complete 10 lines in game B	
3	AISEGYIZ	Must complete 50 lines in game B	
4	EASEGYIZ	Must complete 80 lines in game B	
5	PASAUPPE	Faster 'forced' fall rate	

Remember that you can pick'n'mix your codes! You could try TET Codes 1, 4 and 5 together for the ultimate Tetris test!

Tetris is a trademark of V/O Electronorgtechnica (Elorg). Used by Nintendo of America Inc. under license

146

Thundercade™ Game

If you've never made it to the fortress and saved the world, then these codes are sure gonna help! You can have infinite lives, infinite missiles and infinite bombs with CADE Codes 1, 5 and 6. If you HAVE saved the world, then try doing it again after entering CADE Code 2—bet you can't do it again!

CADE CODE	KEY IN . . .	EFFECT . . .	
1	GXVYPZVI	Infinite lives	
2	PAOYIILA	Start with 1 life	
3	TAOYIILA	Start with 6 lives	
4	PAOYIILE	Start with 9 lives	
5	AAUNLIPP	Infinite missiles	
6	GZXYZTVI	Infinite bombs	
7	TENNPZLA	Start with double bombs	
8	PENNPZLE	Start with triple bombs	
9	ZANYGSZA	Autofire!	

Remember that you can pick'n'mix your codes! You can enter up to THREE separate codes at one time.

Thundercade is a trademark of American Sammy Corporation.

Tiger Heli™ Game

There are lots of interesting Game Genie™ codes for Tiger Heli™—a lot of them are concerned with extra lives, but if you look towards the end of the list you should find a juicy little number that really appeals to you.

HELI CODE	KEY IN . . .	EFFECT . . .	
1	SZSYAEGK	Don't take damage	
2	SLXLGNVS	Infinite lives—1-player game	
3	AEUUYTZA	Start with 2 lives—1-player game	
4	AEUUYTZE	Start with 9 lives—1-player game	
5	SUKLINVS + SUVULNVS	Infinite lives—both players	
6	IASUYYZA	Start with 6 lives—player 1 in a 2-player game	
7	AASUYYZE	Start with 9 lives—player 1 in a 2-player game	
8	IANLZYZA	Start with 6 lives—player 2	
9	AANLZYZE	Start with 9 lives—player 2	
10	LASNVVZA	Extra life every 5 bonus blocks	
11	XTVLUEZK	Start with 2 little-helis after dying	

refer to pages 10 and 11 for instructions. If you still have problems, call 1-513-868-8835.

147

12	TEKNAXIA	Autofire capability
13	ZEKNAXIA	Burstfire capability
14	GXVNZLZP	Turbo boost

Remember that you can pick'n'mix your codes! You can enter up to THREE separate codes at one time, or HELI Code 5 and one other HELI Code.

Tiger Heli is a trademark of Taito America Corporation.
Game Genie is a trademark of Lewis Galoob Toys, Inc.

To The Earth™ Game

Your three wishes are gonna come in handy if you want to make it back to Earth! Use EARTH Code 1 to conserve your energy and try EARTH Code 4 to protect yourself from extraterrestrial attacks along the way. For a mega-difficult game, combine EARTH Codes 3, 6 and 9—only a few hardened shooters will be able to beat that!

EARTH CODE	KEY IN . . .	EFFECT . . .
1	AAEUXTGA	Your shots use up no energy
2	ZAEUXTGA	Your shots use up less energy
3	AAEUXTGE	Your shots use up more energy
4	AEUVEYGP	Enemy bombs do no damage
5	AEUVEYGO	Enemy bombs do half damage
6	AXUVEYGO	Enemy bombs do more damage
7	GOEUEVZA	Bonus energy for shooting enemy
8	GEEUEVZA	Less energy for shooting enemy
9	AEEUEVZA	No energy for shooting enemy

To The Earth is a trademark of Nintendo of America, Inc.

Toobin'™ Game

We've got lots of level warps (TOOB Codes 10 thru 13), codes to give you extra cans (TOOB Codes 6 and 7), codes to give you extra lives, and TOOB Code 9, which gives you turbo-powered left and right movement. What more could you ask for?

TOOB CODE	KEY IN . . .	EFFECT . . .
1	SXUTGIVG	Infinite lives
2	PAOTZTLA	Start with 2 lives
3	TAOTZTLA	Start with 6 lives
4	PAOTZTLE	Start with 9 lives
5	SZEZZIVG	Infinite cans
6	ZPOTTTTA	Start with 18 cans
7	GAOTTTTE	Start with 12 cans
8	PAOTTTTA	Start with 1 can
9	ALKXTAAZ + ALVXLAAZ	Turbo left and right movement
10	PAOZEAAA	Start on level 2
11	LAOZEAAA	Start on level 4
12	IAOZEAAA	Start on level 6
13	YAOZEAAA	Start on level 8

Some codes may cause undesired effects (which are not permanent). If this occurs,

Remember, you can program your own codes! TOOB Codes 6 through 8 might make good codes to try your programming luck on!

Toobin' is a trademark of Atari Games. Used by Tengen under license.

Top Gun™ Game

To make Top Gun™ you've got to be smart. And how's this for size: with TOP Codes 2 thru 4, when you select the usual amount of missiles pre-flight, you sucker the ground crew into loading up TWICE as many by the time you get to the cockpit! You can also warp to any mission by using one of TOP Codes 8 thru 10.

TOP CODE	KEY IN . . .	EFFECT . . .	
1	GXKIKIVG	Infinite missiles	
2	ASEKTOAZ	Take off with double Hound missiles	
3	AXEKYPGO	Take off with double Wolf missiles	
4	GOOGAOZA	Take off with double Tiger missiles	
5	GXUSNGVG	Infinite fuel	
6	IANKLOZA	Start with half fuel	
7	AEKSNLLA	Immune to bullets (but not missiles!)	
8	ZAEGLPPA	Start on mission 2	
9	LAEGLPPA	Start on mission 3	
10	GAEGLPPA	Start on mission 4	

Remember that you can pick'n'mix your codes! You can enter up to THREE separate codes at one time.

Top Gun is a trademark of Paramount Pictures Corporation. Used by Konami Inc. under license.

Top Gun™ (The Second Mission) Game

As well as being able to award yourself extra lives, you can also choose codes to give you extra missiles—you can start a one-player game with 60 Phoenix missiles by using GUN Code 7, or start a two-player game with 20 Phoenix missiles by using GUN Code 8.

GUN CODE	KEY IN . . .	EFFECT . . .	
1	SZVYLIVG	Infinite lives	
2	PASYALLA	Start with 1 life	
3	TASYALLA	Start with 6 lives	
4	PASYALLE	Start with 9 lives	
5	AAKEUYPA	Infinite missiles—1-player game	
6	AENAZIPA	Infinite missiles—2-player game	
7	KUVZTIKO	60 Phoenix missiles—1-player game	
8	KOVXTISA	20 Phoenix missiles—2-player game	

Remember that you can pick'n'mix your codes—you can enter up to THREE separate GUN Codes at the same time.

Top Gun is a trademark of Paramount Pictures Corporation. Used by Konami Inc. under license.

Trojan™ Game

The energy boost codes are probably the most interesting for this game—they make it a bit easier, but not as simple to complete as if you used infinite lives. Try first using TRO Code 7 for a moderate energy boost, and if you feel you need more then use TRO Code 8. You should now be able to beat your current high score easily!

TRO CODE	KEY IN . . .	EFFECT . . .	
1	PENKXPLA	Start with 1 life—player 1	
2	PAOKNZLA	Start with 1 life—player 2	
3	TENKXPLA	Start with 6 lives—player 1	
4	TAOKNZLA	Start with 6 lives—player 2	
5	PENKXPLE	Start with 9 lives—player 1	
6	PAOKNZLE	Start with 9 lives—player 2	
7	YASGUUAE	Start with an energy boost	
8	TPSGUUAE	Start with a super energy boost	
9	GASGUUAA	Start with half usual energy	
10	PASKELZA	Set timer to 1:00	
11	GXEPGKVS	Freeze timer	

Remember that you can pick'n'mix your codes! You can enter up to THREE separate codes at one time.
Trojan is a trademark of Capcom USA, Inc.

Twin Cobra™ Game

All those special weapons that you've picked up are yours to keep if you use COBRA Code 16, while COBRA Code 2 will give you the last word in mass destruction. Use COBRA Code 15 against the enemy some time—it'll make your day!

COBRA CODE	KEY IN . . .	EFFECT . . .	
1	SZVSGXVK	Infinite lives	
2	SZNYXOVK	Infinite bombs	
3	AEUGZIZA	Start with 1 life	
4	IEUGZIZA	Start with 6 lives	
5	AEUGZIZE	Start with 9 lives	
6	AANKLTZA	Start with 1 life after a continue	
7	IANKLTZA	Start with 6 lives after a continue	
8	AANKLTZE	Start with 9 lives after a continue	
9	AAKKYTPA	Infinite continues	
10	PEOKIIIE	9 continues	
11	ZAEGKILE	Start with 9 bombs	
12	GPEGKILA	Start with 20 bombs	
13	ZANIAZLE	9 bombs after dying	
14	GPNIAZLA	20 bombs after dying	

Some codes may cause undesired effects (which are not permanent). If this occurs,

15	AAOYVOLP	Autofire	
16	GZNITZSA	Keep weapon type after death	
17	GZNSAZSA	Keep super chargers after death	

Remember, you can program your own codes! COBRA Codes 11 and 12 might make good codes to try your programming luck on!

Twin Cobra is a trademark of American Sammy Corporation.

Twin Eagle™ Game

There are some brilliant codes for infinite lives and never losing weapons for this fun game! As well as being able to select how many lives you want, TWIN Codes 5 and 6 give you infinite bombs after your first pick-up . . . zzzzooooom!! BANG!

TWIN CODE	KEY IN . . .	EFFECT . . .	
1	SXOSVPVG	Infinite lives—player 1	
2	YEETIPLA	Start with 7 lives—both players	
3	GEETIPLA	Start with 4 lives—both players	
4	PEETIPLA	Start with 1 life—both players	
5	SXNSXSVK	Infinite bombs on pick-up—player 1	
6	SZSIXNVK	Infinite bombs on pick-up—player 2	
7	EYKVVUSA + YAKVNLKZ	Never lose weapons—player 1	
8	ENXVKUSA + YEXVSLSZ	Never lose weapons—player 2	
9	PAEKXTLA	Player 1 has 1 life after a continue	
10	GAEKXTLA	Player 1 has 4 lives after a continue	
11	YAEKXTLA	Player 1 has 7 lives after a continue	

Remember that you can pick'n'mix your codes! You can enter up to THREE separate codes at one time, or one double-code (like TWIN Code 7) and one single code (like TWIN Code 1).

Twin Eagle is a trademark of Romstar Incorporated.

Urban Champion™ Game

With the help of your Game Genie™ you should be able to get a lot more out of this game. You can use URB Code 1 or 2 to improve your punching ability—you can do a lot more damage with each punch. Unfortunately for you, these codes work for your opponent too, whether human or the computer! URB Code 5 lets you throw punches without losing any stamina, making you a more dangerous fighter.

URB CODE	KEY IN . . .	EFFECT . . .	
1	AEEIZGGE	Powerful quick punches	
2	TOEIZGGA	Super powerful quick punch	

refer to pages 10 and 11 for instructions. If you still have problems, call 1-513-868-8835.

3	GZOTZLVG	Freeze the timer	
4	LENVTZTA	Speed up the timer	
5	AAXSLLPA	Become a stronger fighter	
6	LAXSLLPA	Become a weaker fighter	

Remember that you can pick'n'mix your codes! You can enter up to THREE separate codes at one time.

Urban Champion is a trademark of Nintendo of America Inc.
Game Genie is a trademark of Lewis Galoob Toys, Inc.

Vindicators™ Game

Alright Supertanks—let's go! Enter these mega-codes to get extra tank powers! With 14 alien space stations to destroy, you'll find these codes (especially VIND Code 1) a great help!

VIND CODE	KEY IN ...	EFFECT ...	
1	KLUAGTVI	Infinite lives	
2	AAKKYTZA	Start with 1 life	
3	IAKKYTZA	Start with 6 lives	
4	AAKKYTZE	Start with 9 lives	
5	AAUKYTZO + VIKGPTEI	Start with 80 shots	
6	AAUKYTZO + KIKGPTEI	Start with 80 bombs	
7	VYUKEIVI	Automatic fuel replenishment	
8	GZOEVXON	Never lose stars	
9	VVVAAPSA	Start with 10 stars	
10	ZAUKYTZP	Quicker shot re-load	
11	AZKGYVAA	Start with increased shot range	
12	LPKKLVGE	Turbo speed	

Remember that you can pick'n'mix your codes! You can enter up to THREE separate codes at one time, or one double-code (like VIND Code 6) and one single code (like VIND Code 10).

Vindicators is a trademark of Atari Games. Used by Tengen under license.

Wheel Of Fortune™ Game

Get set to play the Game Genie™ way! WHEEL Code 2 gives you a few extra seconds to make the right choice between taking a spin or choosing a vowel. Or see if you can solve the whole puzzle in only 20 seconds with WHEEL Code 3! (NOTE: WHEEL Code 1 gives you just 4 seconds to choose a game tactic, but only after the first time you run out of time).

WHEEL CODE	KEY IN ...	EFFECT ...	
1	YENOIAYA + GEKPOAYA	Less time for choosing	
2	YENOIAYE + YEKPOAYE	More time for choosing	
3	GPUUISAZ	Less time to solve	
4	GLUUISAX	More time to solve	

Some codes may cause undesired effects (which are not permanent). If this occurs,

Remember that you can pick'n'mix your codes.

Wheel of Fortune is a trademark of Merv Griffin Enterprises, a unit of Columbia Pictures Entertainment, Inc. Used by Game Tek/IJE, Inc. under license.
Game Genie is a trademark of Lewis Galoob Toys, Inc.

Who Framed Roger Rabbit™ Game

You can change the number of lives with ROG Codes 1 thru 3, or help Eddie™ survive with ROG Codes 4 and 5. ROG Code 8 makes hitting people easier!

ROG CODE	KEY IN . . .	EFFECT . . .	
1	PESSSYLA	1 life	
2	TESSSYLA	6 lives	
3	PESSSYLE	9 lives	
4	SXVOYIVG	Never lose a life except in Punch lines	
5	SZSZXYVG	Never lose a life in Punch lines	
6	SXKELNVK	Infinite continues	
7	PAUKXTGA	Harder to build strength	
8	EPUKXTGA	Strength to full instantly	

Remember that you can pick'n'mix your codes! You can enter up to THREE separate codes at one time.

Who Framed Roger Rabbit and Eddie are trademarks of The Walt Disney Company and Amblin Entertainment, Inc. Used by LJN Toys, Ltd., under license.

Wild Gunman™ Game

As well as extra lives, you have codes to adjust the number of baddies you have to shoot to finish each level—use WILD Code 9 to have half the number of baddies on each level. You can also start with more ammunition if you use WILD Codes 6 or 7.

WILD CODE	KEY IN . . .	EFFECT . . .	
1	GZOGVYVG	Infinite lives	
2	YEUISPLE + PENGVALA	Start with 1 life	
3	ZEUISPLE + ZENGVALE	Start with 10 lives	
4	YEUISPLE + YENGVALE	Start with 15 lives	
5	GZNIPAVG	Infinite bullets	
6	AXVIEOYA	Start with double normal bullets	
7	AUVIEOYA	Start with triple normal bullets	
8	AEVIEOYE	Start with half normal bullets	
9	IENSUOZA + IEUSSUZA	Shoot 5 baddies to finish level	

Remember that you can pick'n'mix your codes! You can enter up to THREE separate codes at one time,or one double-code (like WILD Code 4) and one single code (like WILD Code 6).

Wild Gunman is a trademark of Nintendo of America Inc.

refer to pages 10 and 11 for instructions. If you still have problems, call 1-513-868-8835.

153

Willow™ Game

Journey with Willow™ on his quest to stop the evil Bavmorda™. With the help of the Game Genie,™ it may just be possible! WILO Code 1 is really helpful—Willow can use magic without losing his magic points. WILO Code 3 gives you all the available items, which is always a good start to anybody's adventures.

WILO CODE	KEY IN . . .	EFFECT . . .	
1	ZASEGOUI	Infinite magic	
2	TGNILGSA	Don't take any hits	
3	XZKYILKP + AVUOXSOZ	Start with all items	
4	GEKISVZA + PNKINTSL	Start at xp level 5	
5	PEKISVZE + PNKINTSL	Start at xp level 10	
6	TEKISVZE + PNKINTSL	Start at xp level 15	

Remember that you can pick'n'mix your codes! You can enter up to THREE separate codes at one time, or one double-code (like WILO Code 3) and one single code (like WILO Code 2).

Willow and Bavmorda are trademarks of LucasFilm, Ltd. Used by Capcom USA, Inc., under license.
Game Genie is a trademark of Lewis Galoob Toys, Inc.

Wizards and Warriors™ Game

If you want to get further and explore more in this game, you could try WIZ Code 1 to 4. Or to make things a little more challenging, try WIZ Code 6. We always felt that the effects of potions don't last long enough . . . well, using WIZ Code 5 and your Game Genie™, you can make sure that they last a bit longer!

WIZ CODE	KEY IN . . .	EFFECT . . .
1	GXVUZGVG	Infinite lives
2	IAUUKAZA + IAXGGAZA	Start with 6 lives
3	AAUUKAZE + AAXGGAZE	Start with 9 lives
4	GZNVILST	Infinite energy
5	NTEINNYK	Potions will last longer
6	PEEVAGZA	Gain half energy value from meat
7	GEEVAGZA	Gain double energy value from meat

Remember, you can program your own codes! WIZ Codes 2 and 3 might make good codes to try your programming luck on!

Wizards & Warriors are trademarks of Acclaim Entertainment, Inc.
Game Genie is a trademark of Lewis Galoob Toys, Inc.

World Cup™ Game

Here's your chance to play in the greatest soccer event in the world, and also to change it to suit your style! CUP Codes 1 thru 6 are self-explanatory. CUP Code 7 will give you a fast-paced game, and for super shots, check out CUP Code 8.

CUP CODE	KEY IN . . .	EFFECT . . .
1	AAUVKZLA	1 minute in tournament mode
2	IAUVKZLA	6 minutes in tournament mode

Some codes may cause undesired effects (which are not permanent). If this occurs,

3	AAUVKZLE	9 minutes in tournament mode
4	IAKTXXPA	6 minutes in match mode
5	ZAKTXXPA	3 minutes in match mode
6	AAKTXXPA	1 minutes in match mode
7	PEXLUIAA	Faster players
8	AYXXNXAL	More powerful 'normal' shots

Remember that you can pick'n'mix your codes. You can enter up to THREE separate codes at one time.
World Cup is a trademark of Technos Japan Corp.

World Wrestling™ Game

You can adjust your training time by using these WORLD Codes. But can you get yourself fit enough to win the TWW™ championship belt?

WORLD
CODE   KEY IN . . .   EFFECT . . .

| 1 | IEUSTOZA | Half training time allowed |
| 2 | GOUSTOZA | Double training time allowed |

World Wrestling and TWW are a trademarks of Tecmo, Inc.

Wrath of the Black Manta™ Game

Using your Game Genie™, you can ensure that you don't die from falling off the screen—use MANT Code 3. MANT Code 4 is also useful—it greatly improves your jumping ability when you're standing still, but it only works after the first time you jump when you start an area.

MANT
CODE   KEY IN . . .   EFFECT . . .

1	AEOAZTLE	Start with extra energy
2	SXSLXUVK	Take no damage from most enemies
3	SZVOKEVK	Never die from falling off screen
4	GZUZSUSO	Mega-jump when stationary
5	AEOAYTZA	Start with 1 life
6	IEOAYTZA	Start with 6 lives
7	AEOAYTZE	Start with 9 lives

Remember that you can pick'n'mix your codes—you can enter up to THREE separate MANT Codes at the same time.
Wrath of the Black Manta is a trademark of Taito America Corporation.
Game Genie is a trademark of Lewis Galoob Toys, Inc.

Wrecking Crew™ Game

Remember to use CREW Code 1 and CREW Code 2 together if you want both players to have infinite lives—it doesn't matter what order you put them into the Game Genie™; as long as they are both entered, both players will have infinite lives.

CREW

CODE	KEY IN . . .	EFFECT . . .
1	SXGXGL	Infinite lives—player 1
2	SXIXZL	Infinite lives—player 2
3	PELXYP	Start with 1 life—both players
4	PELXYO	Start with 10 lives—both players
5	YELXYO	Start with 15 lives—both players

Wrecking Crew is a trademark of Nintendo of America Inc.
Game Genie is a trademark of Lewis Galoob Toys, Inc.

X-Men™ Game

A few codes here for those X-Men™! X Code 1 should prove to be an x-cellent aid to your mission. But, the rest of the X Codes will serve to weaken your X-Men. Is this the work of the forces of evil? Will you still be able to battle it out?

X

CODE	KEY IN . . .	EFFECT . . .
1	SXEEXIST	Infinite energy
2	GVUZPOEG	Half energy for Wolverine™
3	GVUZYOEG	Half energy for Cyclops™
4	PKUXIPXA	Half energy for Nightcrawler™
5	YSKZLOVU	Half energy for Iceman™
6	YNKXPONN	Half energy for Colossus™
7	ASKXYPEZ	Half energy for Storm™

X-Men, Wolverine, Cyclops, Nightcrawler, Iceman, Colossus and Storm are trademarks of Marvel Entertainment Group, Inc.

Xenophobe™ Game

Check out some wicked warping with XENO Codes 5 thru 8. If one player is better than the other, XENO Code 3 is a handy handicap. XENO Code 4 keeps you from picking up any energy, so be careful— things are gonna be a whole lot tougher!

XENO

CODE	KEY IN . . .	EFFECT . . .
1	LASIZOPA	Increase starting energy for both players
2	AAKIYNUT	Infinite energy for both players
3	LAVILONY + AIVIIOGI	More energy to player 1 only
4	SXNITVOO	No energy pickups allowed
5	TAKSAPYA	Start at level 2
6	IAKSAPYA	Start at level 3
7	GAKSAPYA	Start at level 4
8	LAKSAPYA	Start at level 5

Remember that you can pick'n'mix codes. Enter up to THREE separate codes at one time or try one double code (XENO Code 3) and one single code (like XENO Code 5).

Xenophobe is a trademark of Bally Midway Manufacturing used by Sunsoft Corporation of America under license.

Some codes may cause undesired effects (which are not permanent). If this occurs,

Xevious™ The Avenger Game

Everybody knows it's pronounced 'zee-vi-us', don't they? Then again, maybe it isn't—that's just what my buddies say. Anyway, however you say it, the codes remain the same—and here we have a few Game Genie™ babies that will let you select how many lives you start the game with.

ZEV

CODE	KEY IN . . .	EFFECT . . .	
1	SZLNZY	Infinite lives	👪
2	PAZYOG	Start with 1 life	
3	TAZYOG	Start with 6 lives	👪
4	PAZYOK	Start with 9 lives	

Xevious is a trademark of Namco Ltd.
Game Genie is a trademark of Lewis Galoob Toys, Inc.

Xexyz™ Game

Lots of codes here to help you save the land of Xexyz™ from Goruza™! You can alter your number of lives with XEX Codes 3 thru 7. You can also protect yourself against enemy bullets and attacks from mechanical monsters with XEX Codes 1 and 2. For a most excellent game, combine XEX Codes 2, 10 and 12!

XEX

CODE	KEY IN . . .	EFFECT . . .	
1	OTNGGYSV	Immune to enemy bullets	🚫
2	OTNGGTSV	Immune to monsters	
3	PAUZTZLA	Start with 1 life	
4	TAUZTZLA	Start with 6 lives	👪
5	PAUZTZLE	Start with 9 lives	
6	SZEXTKVK	Infinite lives	👪
7	PAUXLILA	1 life after continue	👪
8	LAUGUPPA	3 life points gained from life balls	
9	TAUGUPPA	6 life points gained from life balls	🔧
10	PAUGUPPE	9 life points gained from life balls	
11	VTOXAKSE	Become a whirlwind on new life	
12	AAOLPNAA	Start with and keep foot-wing	👁

Xexyz and Goruza are trademarks of Hudson Soft USA, Inc.

Yo! Noid™ Game

Check out this list! NOID Code 5 stops the timer, so you can spend as long as you like on each level. NOID Code 6 gives you as much magic from small scrolls as you get from the big ones. And if you want to start on a higher level, just check out NOID Codes 10 thru 15.

NOID

CODE	KEY IN . . .	EFFECT . . .	
1	AUUIVPZL + AKUSOPZG	Start with 1 life	
2	IUUIVPZL + IKUSOPZG	Start with 6 lives	👪
3	PUUIVPZU + PKUSOPZK	Start with 9 lives	
4	SXKTTUVK + SXKVPUVK	Infinite lives	👪

refer to pages 10 and 11 for instructions. If you still have problems, call 1-513-868-8835.

157

5	SXXLIGVG	Stop timer
6	IAKUVGPA	More magic from small scrolls
7	AEUGSKTZ	Multi-mega-jumps
8	PAXSNZLA	1 continue
9	TAXSNZLA	6 continues
10	ZEVSKPPA	Start on stage 2
11	GEVSKPPA	Start on stage 4
12	TEVSKPPA	Start on stage 6
13	AEVSKPPE	Start on stage 8
14	ZEVSKPPE	Start on stage 10
15	GEVSKPPE	Start on stage 12

Remember that you can pick'n'mix your codes.

Yo! Noid is a trademark of Domino's Pizza, Inc. Used by Capcom U.S.A., Inc. under license.

Zanac™ Game

Buckle up, gamers! Try some of these wicked Game Genie ™ codes for Zanac™—you can change your lives with ZAN Codes 1 thru 3, or use ZAN Codes 5 thru 10 to get yourself some devastating weapons!

ZAN
CODE	KEY IN . . .	EFFECT . . .
1	PEEKOLLA	Start with 1 life
2	TEEKOLLA	Start with 6 lives
3	PEEKOLLE	Start with 9 lives
4	OXEENYVK	Infinite lives
5	PEOPAGAA	Start with Straight Crusher™
6	ZEOPAGAA	Start with Field Shutter™
7	LEOPAGAA	Start with the Circular™
8	GEOPAGAA	Start with the Vibrator™
9	IEOPAGAA	Start with the Rewinder™
10	TEOPAGAA	Start with the Plasma Flash™
11	YEOPAGAA	Start with rapid fire!

Remember you can pick'n'mix your codes! For an easy ride try combining ZAN Codes 4 and 11.

Zanac, Straight Crusher, Field Shutter, Circular, Vibrator, Rewinder and Plasma Flash are trademarks of FCI, Inc.
Game Genie is a trademark of Lewis Galoob Toys Inc.

Zelda II: The Adventures of Link™ Game

Here's a brilliant set of Game Genie™ codes for the second great Zelda adventure. ZEL Code 5 gives Link™ mega-jump, and Codes 6 thru 10 let you trade the easier-to-get Shield spell for some other useful spells. (The display will still show you have the Shield spell, but you will have the powers of the other spell.)

ZEL2
CODE	KEY IN . . .	EFFECT . . .
1	SZKGKXVK	Link™ has infinite lives

158

Some codes may cause undesired effects (which are not permanent). If this occurs,

2	PASKPLLA	Link starts with 1 life
3	TASKPLLA	Link starts with 6 lives
4	PASKPLLE	Link starts with 9 lives
5	AZUOLIAL	Mega-jump
6	OYKEEVSA + NPKEOVVA	Swap Shield spell for Fire spell
7	LYKEEVSA + VAKEOVVE	Swap Shield spell for Spell spell
8	LZKEEVSA + OPKEOVVA	Swap Shield spell for Fairy spell
9	IIKEEVSE + VAKEOVVE	Swap Shield spell for Life spell
10	VTKEEVSA + OPKEOVVA	Swap Shield spell for Thunder spell

Remember that you can pick'n'mix your codes!

Zelda II: The Adventures of Link and Link are trademarks of Nintendo of America Inc.
Game Genie is a trademark of Lewis Galoob Toys, Inc.

refer to pages 10 and 11 for instructions. If you still have problems, call 1 513 868 8835

159

VIDEO GAME **ENHANCER**

SUBSCRIBE NOW!
GAME GENIE™ UPDATES
You can get codes for many popular new games not found in the Codebook!

Through this exclusive service to Game Genie™ video game enhancer owners, you can get Code Updates you can use to customize many popular games released after the Game Genie Programming Manual and Codebook was printed.

Subscribe now and you'll get four quarterly Code Update issues for **only $3.50** plus $1.50 postage and handling.

HERE'S HOW:
Fill out the coupon and mail it to the address shown on the coupon, along with a check or money order for $5.00 plus your local sales tax. You'll receive four quarterly issues by mail.

ALLOW 8 - 10 WEEKS TO RECEIVE FIRST MAILING.

- -

Game Genie™ Code Update Order Form
Please fill in all information and print clearly.
Yes, I want to subscribe and receive my four quarterly issues.

LAST NAME_____ FIRST NAME _____

ADDRESS _____

CITY_____ STATE _____ ZIP_____
ZIP CODE MUST BE GIVEN

Send a check or money order only, made payable to Game Genie Updates.

Mail to:

**GAME GENIE UPDATES
P.O. BOX 5606
STACY, MN 55079**

ALLOW 8 - 10 WEEKS TO RECEIVE FIRST MAILING.

SUBSCRIPTION PRICE:	**$ 3.50**
POSTAGE & HANDLING:	**$ 1.50**
YOUR STATE SALES TAX*:	**$ _____**
TOTAL ENCLOSED:	**$ _____**

*IMPORTANT: YOU MUST INCLUDE YOUR STATE SALES TAX